And Then?
And Then?
What Else?

ALSO BY DANIEL HANDLER

Novels

Bottle Grove

All the Dirty Parts

We Are Pirates

Why We Broke Up

Adverbs

Watch Your Mouth

The Basic Eight

Not Novels

Weather, Weather

Hurry Up and Wait

Girls Standing on Lawns

As Lemony Snicket

Poison for Breakfast

All the Wrong Questions,
four-book sequence with accoutrements

A Series of Unfortunate Events,
thirteen-book sequence with accoutrements

Swarm of Bees

Goldfish Ghost

29 Myths on the Swinster Pharmacy

The Dark

13 Words

The Composer Is Dead

The Lump of Coal

The Latke Who Couldn't Stop Screaming

And Then?

And Then?

What Else?

DANIEL HANDLER

aka LEMONY SNICKET

Liveright Publishing Corporation

*A Division of W. W. Norton & Company
Independent Publishers Since 1923*

CONTENTS

And Then?

And Then?

What Else?

1

What am I doing?

What am I doing? I am sitting in a café in San Francisco, making things up and writing things down. At my table is an emptied espresso cup, a half-full bottle of fizzy water, some index cards with words and phrases typed on them, and a bright yellow legal pad on which I am writing with a pen while an unsharpened pencil rolls around for fiddling with. As always, there's a book with me hardly anyone has read. Today it is a book called *We Both Laughed in Pleasure*. I'm hunched over, headphoned; I look like a lunatic, which is likely the wrong word. It feels right, though. I like how the word sounds, *lunatic*, and I like its slightly old-fashioned tincture, which makes its wrongness less wrong to my ears, like calling someone a *jackal* or a *wench*. But what do I know? Look at me: I am staring at nothing, trying to think of the word for what it is I resemble here in the café.

No wonder people ask me all the time what I am doing, and the answer is embarrassing: I am making things up and writing them down. For instance, when I said that people ask me all the time what am I doing, I made that up. Here, as all over the world, people generally ignore one another. In twenty years of working like this in cafés, I have been asked what I am doing precisely twice. Both times the people assumed I was a teacher. I told them yes, I'm a teacher, because it was too embarrassing to say, no, I am not a teacher; I am making things up and writing them down. But I like to imagine that lots of people ask, or at least wonder, what it is I am doing.

"Why don't you write at your desk?" is another thing I imagine people ask me, although they never do. It is true I have a very nice desk. The man who sold it to me said it was originally a medical examining table. If that's true—and why would he make it up?—then it used to have undressed people on it, sitting or lying down on those big sheets of paper that look like where an artist might sketch out a mural, or so I imagine. Now different things are sitting there. Some of the things I like, such as books I am reading or still thinking about or can't wait to read, and a few paperweights that feel good to hold. But some things on my desk I am trying to avoid, tedious chores that I have put on my desk so I cannot avoid them. And of course there is a computer on my desk, where I type what I write down on legal pads. But the computer is also full of dull chores—correspondence and business and whatnot, plus the internet and its harrowing distractions. So I leave the house. I do not bring my computer, not only because I am trying to avoid it, but because I do not know what to do with it in the café when I need the bathroom. I could ask a stranger to watch it for me, like a fool, or bring it with me, feeling like a pervert while trying to balance the computer precariously on top of the toilet to keep it safe. You can leave a legal pad and some index cards on a table. No one will steal them, because they think you are a lunatic.

Sometimes, on my way out of the house, I look back at my office and think, as if gazing fondly at an infant in a crib, *it looks like a little angel when it's sleeping.* This is a quote from an old comic strip called *Cathy*, by Cathy Guisewhite. *Cathy* was a daily comic strip that ran for thirty-four years, which I read occasionally as a child though never particularly liked. Cathy, *Cathy*'s heroine, once said this about her busy desk. I would guess I was twelve when I read it. I do not know why that line has stayed in my head all this time. It is not especially pleasing for me when I write it down or say it out loud. I would guess Guisewhite has long forgotten it. But it has lived, and lives still, in my mind and my mouth. I suppose it could be said that this line is a literary reference, especially now that I am putting it in a book. But that's not right, not really. I realized not long ago that that line is something I think, even say out loud sometimes, when I look at my desk. So it's typed here on an index card, *it looks like a little angel when it's sleeping,* so I could have it here with me in this café, and write it down.

I am not remarkable in this way, having these things in my head. We're all wandering around thinking about some little thing at any given moment, something which everyone else has most likely forgotten. Some of these things we get to say out loud—incidents from our own lives or little bits from culture which we use to illustrate some point or use as an example—though most of them just stay in our heads, too private or just not interesting enough for anyone else. It is remarkable that I have the astonishing luck to do this for a living, to have this nonsense count as work.

But that is not a sufficient explanation for what it is I am doing. It is not just work. Many writers refer to what they do as a calling, which never sounds right to me. It's too grandiose, too literary, to talk about literature that way; the more an author refers to writing as a calling, the less likely I am to be interested in their work. Many of my favorite writers cannot even use literary terms to describe whatever it is they are working on. "I am working on a *thing*," is what they say, when cornered, these people who work with words, who when called upon to produce a noun, reach for the least specific one. *Thing.* This is what I am doing, some *thing*, in this café. In another astonishing bit of luck, I got to interview the writer Rachel Ingalls, perhaps my absolute favorite writer, at what turned out to be very near the end of her life. She referred to what she did as *a compulsion*. As always with Ingalls, it's a little dark but very good. Lunatics are compulsive. No one has asked me to do what I am doing, not really. There is a great, great heap of literature in the world, and even though most of it is awful, there's still more than enough good stuff—*way* more than enough—to last anyone's lifetime. When I add to this gargantuan heap, I have a small hope that someone will find it interesting, but there's no sensible argument that the world needs another book, by me or anyone else. But I'm doing it anyway. I can't really stop and I don't really want to.

The most visible example of what I do, some little scrap of culture living in my head and becoming something else, is the poetry of Charles Baudelaire, of course. I have written a bunch of books about orphans named Baudelaire. This is because when I was young, about the same time as *it looks like a little angel when it's sleeping*, I discovered a copy of Baudelaire's *The Flowers of Evil* in my local library. I knew what it was at once. The title of the book made it perfectly clear: It was a horror novel. Although the real title, something in French, was printed on the cover, the library had written the English translation on a small piece of paper and taped it helpfully over *Les Fleurs du Mal*. I know this is true because I went back to this book, the same copy, over and over, long after I knew I was wrong about what it was. I didn't get my own copy until I was in college, and by then it was much too late. I was already hopelessly lost to a relationship with Baudelaire and the kind of literature he made up and wrote down, the kind of literature I like—strange literature, the best literature.

But I was twelve when I found it first. I know this because of the publication date of the edition, 1982, and *The Flowers of Evil* was in the section of the library which featured newly published books. I didn't know that then. I was puzzled by this section of the library, which had a small handful of books, face out instead of shelved properly in a row of spines, books which had nothing in common as far as I could tell. There must have been a placard placed someplace—"New Arrivals" or something—but I didn't see it, or didn't care to see it. Something that looms so large now in my professional life—who has a new book, when is it coming out—was, when I was a child, something rightfully ignored. I thought—I *preferred* to think—that libraries just sometimes liked to draw attention to some books they were thinking about for no particular reason. *The Flowers of Evil* looked good, so I took it home to read.

Stupidity, delusion, selfishness and lust
torment our bodies and possess our minds,
and we sustain our affable remorse
the way a beggar nourishes his lice.

I have no memory of the first time I read this first stanza of the first poem in *The Flowers of Evil*. It's a memory I wish I had, opening a book I thought would be something like the spooky books by Stephen King or V. C. Andrews I read sometimes, or the more gothic fare by M. R. James or Anne Radcliffe that I'd find later. I don't know if these lines produced some epiphanic moment. I doubt it. It was something much slower than that. The poems nagged me, and I went back to the library and found the book again—soon afterward, and over and over. I could make it up, some wide-eyed story of gasping at my first reading, but really I can only guess that what struck me about these lines then is what strikes me now. I wouldn't have had words for it then. Now, I would say that Baudelaire invites a grotesque culpability, that you cannot read *The Flowers of Evil* without being a participant in it. So much poetry makes the case that the world is beautiful, and seeks to remind us that we're connected to this beauty. That was likely the poetry I was encountering in school at the time. I don't remember any of that poetry, not even hating it. It failed to connect with me at all. Age twelve puts me in sixth or seventh grade, at a large public middle school, underfunded and ugly—the school, I mean, although like anyone that age I was uncomfortable in my own skin, and so unlikely to be persuaded by claims that we were all pretty. This startling rejoinder, that instead we were tormented by stupidity, delu-

6

sion, selfishness and lust, surely spurred some delicious startle. I likely would have blurred past "affable remorse," a phrase that's still something of a puzzle to me even now when I know what both those words mean, but "the way a beggar nourishes his lice" would have stuck with me. Homelessness was becoming more and more visible then, in San Francisco and nationwide—the naming of a problem, reframed as a social issue rather than, say, the dismissive use of the word "bum." I'd begun to visit the main branch of the San Francisco Public Library, which had a sizable number of unhoused visitors, and I have a memory of seeing someone with bugs on their person. Lice had made their way once or twice through the schools I attended, and I'd had the chemical rinses and the other hullabaloo that came with a classroom outbreak. But here were people out and about with lice, or whatever they were, the special shampoos and combs impossibly out of reach, a population glaringly visible to library patrons but hardly to be found in poetry. San Francisco is the first library system to hire a full-time social worker as part of the library staff, and that mission, a Venn diagram in which rarefied literature and social services overlap under the idea of accessibility, surely had some effect on me, however sub- or unconscious, as a frequent patron who ended up bringing the name *Baudelaire* to all sorts of readers.

Was all this in my mind as I read one line of bewildering poetry at twelve? Don't be ridiculous. But something started there, some *thing*. It is bigger than the little slot in which *it looks like an angel when it's sleeping* fits, ready to be called up whenever I look at my desk. It is not just that Baudelaire took up residence—*permanent* residence, as far as I can tell—in my mind, bumping up against other things until it was time for me to do something with them. Reading Baudelaire made a new space, a different world than the one I thought I was in. I wasn't in the library, or at home on the floor of my room or in bed— wherever I first opened the book to read. I was somewhere else, a place I liked better, in which I was not just reading but participating. It is a space all readers know from childhood, when you're not just enjoying a book but sort of inside it, joining the story. You're standing next to the hero, maybe, or the hero is you. The adventure is yours, even as it is only in a book you're holding. It's the thing, the space in which literature works, the space in which I move around.

I'm always wary about calling this space a *process*. Some writers like this word, and enjoy speaking openly about it, often at great length, while I wish I could lay my head down on a table. It is true that some things are interesting to see made, and do visit the Murano glass factory when you next get to Venice. But lots of things aren't. I was once at a long fancy table in the middle of a field, eating things that had all been gathered or farmed or raised in the immediate area, which meant there was a story with each serving of food, a story which interrupted conversation between people at the table, so that no one would miss the details of the lamb or the watercress. At the end of the meal, we were invited to see where the strawberries had come from, and I found myself alone at the table. Had the strawberries come out of a volcano, or if they had been painstakingly carved from one enormous strawberry, by an elderly couple in traditional garb, then of course I would have hurried to see it. But I knew they had been gathered from strawberry plants, something I had seen many times, including the failed ones in my own yard, which are dull to look at. Literature, I think, is often like this. I want everyone at the table, talking and feasting, enjoying themselves even as they argue. But I don't want to be led away from the party, to see the ugly strawberry plants, or the barn where the lambs are slaughtered, or wherever watercress comes from.

When I even hear the word *process*, I can only think of a terrible afternoon I spent in a windowless room. After writing nine drafts of a screenplay for the Lemony Snicket movie, I'd been fired, and they'd filmed a script written largely by someone else. There were parts of it, after filming, with which the people making the movie were dissatisfied, and so they called me on the last day of a grueling book tour and asked me if, instead of flying home into the arms of my wife, I would fly to them and tell them what was wrong. I said no. They offered a pile of money and I called my wife and she said, darling, just go. I got on an airplane and then into an automobile, and as the automobile approached my ugly destination, my film agent called me and said that my financial offer had been reduced, while I was in the air, to the amount of zero dollars. I went into the building anyway, wondering what I was doing. Inside, the arguing commenced, interspersed by watching rough edits of scenes of the movie—the first I had seen of it—and one of the people in the room, sitting alone on a little sofa, asking if anyone else felt cold. Nobody did, so as we continued to argue, she took cushions off of the sofa, first the decorative ones, and then the structural ones—the ones you lean against, the ones you sit on—and piled them up on her lap and limbs, for presumptive warmth. Eventually only her head was visible on the top of the pile of cushions, the argument continuing all the while. Finally someone just up and told me that I didn't know what I was talking about, and while I largely agreed with this—then as now, I had no idea how to edit or improve an already-filmed film—I asked why then they had flown me out here to sit in this room. The woman sighed on the sofa. She looked like an igloo, or maybe a ziggurat, with her face at the top where people get sacrificed in offensive adventure movies. I understood then that I was among raving lunatics. Previously I had considered these people innocent, and then maybe dumb, and then maybe a pack of vicious demons. I understood, too, that they were, at least obliquely, the reason I owned a house. But now I saw that to argue with them, to talk with them, to spend time with them, was to spend time with utter, gallivanting, wide-grinned, swerving lunatics, and I was a lunatic, too. It was my own lunatic story they had filmed wrong, and I had entered this windowless room, of my own free will and for no money, to listen to lunatics tell me I was wrong. "Daniel," this lunatic said to me, head atop the cushions, "you have to trust our *process*."

I didn't, of course. And I don't trust my own. I shrink from calling it a process, or calling it a calling. Still, it's not enough to say that stumbling upon a book I liked led to my writing a sequence of books in which the young orphan heroes have the same name as an old French poet. That doesn't explain what I am doing at all. Maybe it's a compulsion, or just a space—a *space* to work on a *thing*. But here is what I do: Little bits from all over the place, mostly literature—scurry into my mind and I scurry after them. They are not original ideas—not because they are not original, although of course they aren't; it's because they're not ideas. Not yet. In the beginning they are just *things*. They're things other people have written, mostly, and so other people have read them before, sometimes lots and lots of people. I think of a friend of mine who told me a story about when he first moved to Los Angeles and complained about the traffic. "People said to me, didn't you know about Los Angeles? Didn't you know the traffic was a problem? And I said yeah, of course I did. But now *it's happening to me*." I'm not the first to encounter these little items, but these little things are happening to *me*. There's nothing to do with them yet. I'm waiting, or they're waiting. The waiting is a crucial part of it, so crucial that it feels like the waiting is more important than anything these things are waiting for.

As with so many things, Toni Morrison has said it better:

> But I can't say that aloud; I can't tell anyone that I have been waiting for this all my life and that being chosen to wait is the reason I can. If I were able I'd say it. Say make me, remake me. You are free to do it and I am free to let you because look, look. Look where your hands are. Now.

These sentences return to me often, as I survey those scraps in my mind. I am not exactly sure what Morrison means. But when this passage is happening to me, it means that I start to get my hands on these things that I keep thinking about, to try to get them into some kind of order. I put them together, so they stop dashing around and start clinging to something. I want to do it quickly but I know I need to take my time, to wait until they start clinging to each other, without my forcing it.

11

A more concrete way of saying this is that I almost always have a notebook in my pocket, and I write little things down in it: scenes or sentences that I remember suddenly, or one right in front of me, bits of literature or conversation or film or music or I don't know. And then I get my hands on them. If I remember some idea from a book, I reread the book like I am taking apart a clock, to figure out how it ticks. In some ways, this ruins the book, but it makes the relationship deeper, more intimate, like seeing someone in the actual clothes they wear to bed, rather than whatever they might have worn to impress you. I write down more things about these things. When the notebook is full, I type it onto my screen and print it out as a document, trying to remember to narrow the margins, because then I cut out all these things from the document and then tape these little strips of paper to index cards. That part feels a little sad, a lunatic thing to do, but I remember the person covered in sofa cushions, my fellow lunatic, and I keep going. I find a flat surface and begin to move these index cards around. Sometimes this feels like doing a jigsaw puzzle, and sometimes it feels like washing clothes by hand, the cards moving, stacking, clumping together. I'm usually listening to music, pieces of music that seem like they want to hang out with these index cards, and it begins to feel more like a party, that I am a host, a little nervous, putting people together in groups in the hopes they get along. And I'm talking with people, too, sort of. I'm remembering my friend Amanda Davis, a writer with the exact same birthday as mine, who said she always tries to find the center of gravity in something she likes, a sentence, a paragraph, a chapter, a novel, the little bit that actually entrances her, when she encountered it. *Center of Gravity*, I've written on blackboards before, when I try to talk about this, pleased to remember Davis, gone now, and also to be reminded that the initials spell "COG." I think of another friend, living years ago in a squat in Brooklyn and showing me how he was installing his own insulation, and my saying it must be hard to learn how to do that, and his answer: That the hard part wasn't learning how to do it; the hard part was doing it. I think of the writer Michelle Tea, saying it's like nursery school: You have to make a mess and you have to clean up, and I think of the song in which Isaac Hayes says, *it ain't how good I make it, baby, it's how I make it good.* A pulse runs underneath my hands, or maybe just in my ears. *And then? And then? What else?*

What am I doing? I'm working now. The index cards are in little piles, like a city block seen from above, not a big city because the piles aren't yet skyscraper-tall, but someplace reasonable, where writers can afford to live. I've put them in order, although the order is still mostly wrong. I think about when my friend was in film school and her instructor told her she didn't have enough footage for her short documentary about the Brooklyn Bridge, and how this filled her with relief, because she didn't want to make a documentary about the Brooklyn Bridge. I want to make the book these cards will make best, not an imaginary assignment in my head. I think of my son, when he was clearing trees with a friend of mine, telling my friend that if it was a smaller tree he could lift it himself, and my friend telling him—or at least, how he told it to me—*well, this is the tree we have.* I think about when I interviewed the poet Heather Christle about her terrific titles ("That Little Bird Was Not OK,"

"Moss Does Not Love Other Moss") and asked who they were for, for her or for the audience, and she said, *for the poems.* I think about a moment in Harpo Marx's autobiography, *Harpo Speaks,* in which he performs a slapstick act for an unimpressed Russian audience, but the next night, when his slapstick is preceded by a short, dramatic scene between two actors, it brings the house down, and I try to think about different kinds of balance, of expectation and surprise. I think of Maira Kalman, the artist with whom I've worked lots of times, telling me she had no imagination, that she only painted real things, she just put them in different places. I think of a cassette I listened to one long teenage summer, which cut off the song "Let's Go to Bed" by the Cure about midway through, so for years I thought that the remarkable things about that song were that it ends suddenly and that it never says "let's go to bed," and neither of those are true. I think about how the film *Irma Vep* ends suddenly, with a scritchy-scratchy coda resembling nothing else in the movie, because why not?

All these things have been canonized in my head. They live there exerting deep influence on my work and on my life. The idea of a literary canon—the important books one should apparently read—is hotly debated, of course, which often feels necessary and/or fun. Voices gain cultural prominence, or lose it, or are blocked from participating, invited or disinvited, prized or banned, and I like listening, occasionally participating, in this conversation in one way or another. But the most important literary canon is one's own—not just a list of favorite books or what have you, but the individual moments, the twists of plot or turns of phrase, the tiny secret reasons you love what you love.

This canon keeps you company, gives you comfort and delight. You can take little bits of it with you when you go sit someplace, and sometimes you can do something with them, aside from just marveling at them for the umpteenth time. I encourage people who want to be writers to delineate and study this canon, their own, above every other. I don't think anyone I tell to do it does it. Everyone has to learn for themselves. Nevertheless, this is how I do it.

I have written these pages the way I write almost everything, on a legal pad, with little arrangements of index cards that say things like "Irma Vep" or "take it apart like a clock," or that sit in books I love marking the places I like best. Today I have with me one marking a passage in *We Both Laughed in Pleasure*, the selected diaries of Lou Sullivan. Sullivan was a writer and an activist, one of the first visible trans men, whose surprising and roundabout journey, recounted in all its heartfelt lunacy, starts about here:

> I'm sure social working is what I want. Yes—the excitement off getting a gun away from a teenage boy. Having to talk to him. I'd love that. Well—my guitar teach (he's 18) asked me if I'm going out with someone or going steady. I said I was only 13. He said so what. I said my mother'd kill me. He said well tell her now listen here. He shook his finger. I want to do that.

What I love about this passage is how the very clear sentences give you the illusion that you can follow the logic, that Sullivan's mind is clear and easily explained, when really he's as lunatic as the rest of us. I stare at this passage, the choppy tug of the sentences and the yearning floating over it. *I want to do that.*

What am I doing? I'm trying to show you this canon in my head. Explaining these bits of literature, the lunatic ways they stay in my mind and influence me, is a more fun, a more exciting, a more *accurate* way of explaining what I've done and what I'm doing. And what am I doing? I am sitting in a café right now, hunched over my legal pad—*and then, and then, what else?*—wondering if the right way to end this paragraph is to say, *here we go.*

2

Tell me more.

Once I was at a party that was particularly bad. It was held in broad daylight, at a house in a desirable community reached via highway, so real estate and traffic were the mandatory conversation topics, and I moved quickly through clusters of people talking about square footage and new exit ramps, trying not to let my eyes roll into the back of my head. I made it all the way to the back porch where some children were hanging around bothering the plants. One, the maybe-six-year-old son of someone I knew was sitting near the ice chest. I said hey and asked him what was up, in the hopes of a better conversation. I got it.

"Last night I dreamed I was a horse," he said.

All my life, I get told I'm a child. Of course, it was true for a while. But when my height and weight made adulthood undeniable, it was something still tossed at me in one form or another. I'm a child at heart. I never really grew up. Childhood, whatever precisely that is, should have departed from my mind, and instead here it is. When I was actually a child, my mother, who remembers this differently, told me what to do if our house caught fire in the middle of the night. This probably would not happen, she said, but if it did, the last thing I would want to do would be to open my bedroom door. Instead, I should press my hands against it, to feel if it was hot. If it was, I should jump out the window. I might break my leg, but breaking my leg was better than the alternative.

I don't know how many times I went to my bedroom door in the middle of the night to see if I should jump out the window. I never jumped—a small miracle for an imaginative child. My bedroom was in the attic—like Anne Frank, I used to think, another Jewish kid who stayed in their room a lot—three floors above a little yard where I would have fallen, probably on the slender lawn but possibly into the neighbor's shrubbery, which had little berries I'd been told were poisonous. But I would more likely land in the grass, and lie there, groaning. I moved my legs in bed, twisting them best I could into broken positions I had learned from cartoons. I couldn't really bend them like the coyote's legs, because mine weren't broken, not yet. I would groan weakly, hoping to attract the attention of the firefighters, the orange glow of my burning house illuminating the poison berries on the lawn. They lay there fallen on the grass all the time, and I used to think about putting them in the blender with some water, or orange juice to mask the taste, but I didn't really have anyone I wanted to poison, nor could I imagine how to get them to drink it. It did occur to me, though, that one or two of the berries could roll their way into my mouth when I landed there, already broken-legged and now poisoned, too. Still, even then, better than the alternative. This is what I think of, when people say I am still a child, moving my legs around, thinking about poisoning people and houses burning down.

One series of children's books I wrote begins with a poisoning; the other starts things off with a house on fire. Naturally I get asked why I think such things are suitable for children. This is very easy to answer. It is because I found them interesting as a child and because I still find them interesting now. All the best literature has such things happening. Texts which have survived for thousands of years, which weren't typed up but inscribed, memorized, or even carved into stone, are about enormous, strange, frightening things. If you had to sum up lasting literature in a single sentence, you could do worse than "I dreamed I was a horse"—prophetic dreams and animal transformations appear much more frequently in the old epics than, say, which neighborhoods have the best schools, for the same reason that it makes better conversation. I like talking to children not because they are children—indeed, that aspect sometimes makes it more difficult—but because they generally have a firmer grasp on what might be interesting to say.

Of course this makes people look at me funny, a grown man talking to children. For all male children's authors this is a familiar accusatory air. (Female children's authors, meanwhile, are presumed sexless and schoolmarmish, even when they're cracking blue jokes and drinking gimlets next to me, which they often are.) The proximity of wickedness to children is something the whole world can't stop thinking about, even though of course most terrible things happen to adults. But children have had less time on Earth, is the argument, so a terrible thing happening is of greater import and impact, or perhaps it is just that children generally seem fragile. When my son was born he felt to me like a bag of blood, to be carried around carefully and fearfully. Suddenly every foreign object, every rough surface or sharp corner, had to be spotted and sorted out before you could put the gurgling bag down anyplace. The hospital wouldn't let us leave with him until they had verified we had the proper car seat, which felt like a sick joke: The danger, clearly, was bringing this baby, this delicate bag of blood, anywhere near an automobile, an obvious and long-proven instrument of slaughter.

Not long before my son was born, a journalist invited me to attend a press screening of a movie marketed to children. The journalist thought it would be a hoot to know what Lemony Snicket thought of it. I spent a few years as a freelance writer, writing (among other forgettable pieces) a handful of snarky movie reviews, so I'd attended enough press screenings that I thought I knew what to expect: a weird corporate room with a few other scruffy critics trying to take notes in the dark. Instead it was a proper movie theater, packed with children who were thrilled to be getting a sneak peek. Before the movie began, the lights lowered for a showing of a lengthy soft drink commercial featuring a pop star, a young woman who has since been understood to have been a prisoner for most of her career, but then just regarded, at an age just a little older than the children in the audience, to be sexy. I'd seen her dance moves before and found them harmless, but on the big screen, or perhaps because of the costume or the young crowd, they seemed more garish, nightmarishly sexual, and a team of lackeys came down the aisles distributing little flags with the logo of the drink. "Myth,

the practice of memory," says the poet Joanna Kyger, and I try
to remind myself that it's entirely possible I am remembering
incorrectly, that we were not actually all told to wave our flags
and chant the name of the drink, the name of the musician, the
name of the movie, over and over. But there it is in my head. It
was shortly after 9/11, and I had recently spent a harrowing
afternoon in a skyscraper conference room in New York, which
had a view of where the towers had once been. I could not stop
looking at the blank space in the landscape outside, while inside
a team of people showed me a slideshow of how they were plan-
ning to get an army of children to attend the Lemony Snicket
movie, which had not been written yet, let alone filmed. "We
can make children get excited about *anything*," said one of the
presenters, and now in the theater for another movie, amidst a
crowd of excited children, my blood ran cold with the knowledge that children were in danger, grave danger, and that I was
part of the danger, culpable and well-paid, which meant, of
course, that I was an adult. I don't think I gave a very good
interview afterward.

Car accidents and aggressive advertising, of course, aren't
what anyone thinks about when they think about danger to
children. They think—*we* think—of abduction, murder, sexual violence—comparatively rare events in real life, but looming large in the imagination. We hold these shadowy evils in
our mind, almost supernatural in their power: Inhuman monsters beckoning to children, whisking them away, performing unspeakable acts on their fragile frames. Where do these
nightmares come from? From the same old stories. This kind of
senseless, horrid violence is more prevalent in the old tales than

anywhere on Earth, along with other improbables like chival-
rous knights, fair-minded kings, conniving witches and venge-
ful ghosts. We don't see these entities much in real life, but we
read about them, over and over, especially as children.

There is a vast pile of commentary seeking to spell out why
such literature has such lasting appeal—a pile that serves as
further testament to the old stories' power. The explanations,
however, are hardly ever convincing. An evangelical Christian writer, for instance, once told me that old stories are full
of dragons because dragons—or, as some secularists prefer to
call them, *dinosaurs*—were then still roaming the earth. Most
of the commentaries, however, are tamer, usually huddling
around some prescriptive benefit, especially for young people.
The archetypical journey of the hero, a misfit at home, setting
off and overcoming various obstacles building toward some
great triumph and reward, is meant to model order, both in its
view of the world and as a suggestion as to how to behave in
it. Be steadfast and true and the world which surrounds you,
even as it seems chaotic and menacing, will treat you kindly
in turn. I won't waste any ink reminding you this is nonsense,
because if you are reading this, you are here in the world and you
already know. But such nonsense also misses why these stories
are appealing, which is not much rooted in the inspiring value of
the hero's journey or the other machinations of the plot—tropes
which are, of course, available elsewhere. Nobody reads old stories to learn how to behave, even if that's the reason they're given
to us. No, the appeal lies in the premise: The bewildering world
presented as the tale begins, astonishingly foreign and, because
the world is astonishingly foreign, very, very familiar.

When I was young, my favorite story in the Brothers Grimm book we had laying around was "The White Snake," which begins like this:

> A long time ago there lived a King whose wisdom was known in all the country. Nothing remained long unknown to him, and it was as if the knowledge of hidden things was brought to him in the air. However, he had one curious custom.

That last sentence slays me with its "however"—*however* he had one curious custom? Is not his supernatural wisdom a little curious? In any case,

> Every day at dinner, after the table had been cleared and everyone gone away, a trusty servant had to bring in one other dish. But it was covered up, and the servant himself did not know what was in it, and no one else knew, for the King waited until he was quite alone before he uncovered the dish. This had gone on a long time, but at last there came a day when the servant could restrain his curiosity no longer, but as he was carrying the dish away he took it into his own room. As soon as he had fastened the door securely, he lifted the cover, and there he saw a white snake lying on the dish.

From here on the story gets less interesting. Our hero the servant takes a bite of the snake—as one would?—and it gives him the power to understand the speech of animals, a skill he uses first to prove his innocence (he is suspected of stealing the Queen's ring, but a duck blabs about swallowing it) and then on his journey, in which he encounters and aids various animals in peril, who then reward him in turn by assisting in various tasks dreamt up by another king—you know the sort of tasks I mean, *pick up these million grains of millet, fetch an apple from the tree of life*—in order to marry the beautiful daughter and live in undisturbed happiness in the story's last paragraph. But all this is ordinary—and comforting, even if you like this sort of thing—next to the deep strangeness of the story's premise: That white snake, brought secretly and consumed nightly. Everything you want to ask—where does the snake come from? how did this get started?—is nowhere to be found in the text, even though what is most indelible about the story is that lifted cover in the locked room, and the snake on the dish—skinned, in my mind's eye, with some parsley and a slice of lemon for garnish. It was what I liked to think about most in a story which is not, remember, called something like "The Guy Who Was Kind to Animals." Whatever moral lesson one might try to attach to the tale falls apart—*be kind to your fellow creatures and your kindness will be repaid*, for instance, would be better presented in a story which does not feature the hero slaughtering various *other* animals in his helpful efforts—but the white snake in "The White Snake" remains stuck in the mind. And this is fairly standard in Grimm Brothers stories, which tend to begin with some odd, spooky premise—a man abandons his children in the woods, a childless woman has a craving for a neighbor's herb, a queen admires her own drops of blood after a household accident—before moving on to

24

a much more standard arc. Many of these odd premises are scrubbed away in the supposedly more child-friendly versions of the stories. But the inexplicable cores of these stories linger nevertheless, so the details we remember most—a talking mirror, little men who work in a mine, a great climbable length of human hair—stick with us no matter what hero's journey tries to hog the spotlight.

It seems timely to mention here, with Rapunzel's lock, that what my mother remembers telling me is not to jump out the window, but to make a long rope out of my blankets to lower myself to the ground.

Why do we like these bewildering premises? Because they're the most realistic parts of the story. When we are small, for example, voices come from all sorts of strange places—all kinds of screens and speakers—which we're likely exposed to before we can talk ourselves, so the idea of a sycophantic mirror fits right in. It is likely we see members of our family go off to work, as mysterious and normalized as a team of mining dwarves. No child who has met more than one other child wonders why everyone is mean to Cinderella. This isn't to suggest that these premises aren't bewildering after all—just that bewilderment is at the heart of being human, and that such familiar narrative arcs as a hero's journey look more like desperate and contrived attempts to turn away from the inescapable inexplicables of being alive. This is why I kept reading, again and again, "The White Snake" when I was young, thinking about this king and his covered dish, and continue to love the strangeness, the strangeness that so strongly resembles life, of the best literature.

The Giantess

Back when prolific Nature birthed large-size
progeny daily, it would have been fun
to live beside some girlish giantess
like a luxurious cat beside a queen
and watch her body blossom with her soul
as she enjoyed her frightful exercise
and fathom if she felt a loving zeal
from the vague moisture swimming in her eyes,
to wander her colossal form at ease
and mount the slopes of her enormous knees,
and, in the summer, when the harsh sun laid
her out, lethargic, over her estate,
to sleep casually in a vast breast's shade
like a quaint village at a mountain's foot.

This is one of the Baudelaire poems which I literally could
not believe when I read it. I could not believe it existed; I could
not believe it was a poem. I've been carrying a copy of it around
town lately, trying to figure out what to say here, and I love showing it to friends, who cannot believe these words are written on
a piece of paper in front of them. The critic Roland Barthes, in
his book *The Pleasure of the Text*—which was so trendy when I
was a student that it took me a while to realize it's actually very
good—talked about a certain kind of writing that "unsettles the
reader's historical, cultural, psychological assumptions, the consistency of his tastes, values, memories, brings to a crisis his relation with language," and well, this poem does the job. I mean,

look at it. One would be hard-pressed to find a poem as stuffed with sexual fetishism as "The Giantess" and still not quite have sexual fetishism be its primary feature, or a poem more misogynist in its creepy, pervy objectification that still manages to be more lunkish than it is objectionable. Again, a great part of this is the premise—"back when prolific nature birthed large-size / progeny daily" is a bewildering white-snake opener if there ever was one. But the way the stanzas move us from the loamy turmoil of bodily fixation—it hardly matters exactly which biological function "her frightful exercise" refers to—to the natural halcyon imagery ("like a quaint village at a mountain's foot) without ever losing sight of the fact that Baudelaire is drooling over a giant woman is its own inscrutable marvel. The poem stuck with me for its sheer impossibility, how it sits in a landscape all its own, resembling no kind of literature or even experience. Well, that isn't quite true. It reminded me of something.

The movie *Attack of the 50 Foot Woman* has been forever linked in my mind to that Baudelaire poem, doubtless because I stumbled upon them both at the same time. In the case of this 1958 film, it was due to a source of serendipity I deeply miss, the local television station matinee, when boredom forces you to watch not whatever you choose from an endless viewing menu, but whatever was found lying around the station that day. That day it was this.

Attack of the 50 Foot Woman is a bad movie. The premise is fairly straightforward—a UFO, driven by a cosmic giant, lands in California, and its radiation causes an unhappily married heiress to grow to guess what size. As with many other monster movies, constraints on budget and imagination mean that there's not much that can happen after the monster arrives, so the movie must play for time as long as it can, with writers and actors not at all up for such a task. In this movie's case, the strategy is to offer a sordid melodrama, snitching scenarios from conniving noirs like *The Postman Always Rings Twice* and histrionic dramas like *Who's Afraid of Virginia Woolf?*, so the viewer fidgets through snarling drunken fights and a half-baked plan to eliminate the heiress for her money, before we're finally treated to the attack. There are a couple of what you might call plot twists—keep your eyes on that silent butler—but the story is so limply executed that it feels like twisting a noodle. The ill-funded visuals mean that much of the trickery—a big papier-mâché hand poking the cast, an extreme close-up of a bald man reaching toward the camera—takes a moment to register: *oh, that's supposed to be her hand, oh, that's supposed to be a giant.*

Still, it works. There's something about it. It unsettles the viewer's historical, cultural, psychological assumptions, the consistency of their tastes, values, memories, and lines like "She will tear up the whole town until she finds Harry, and then she'll tear up Harry" brings to a crisis our relation to language. The movie stuck with me then, and it stuck with me when I watched again some forty years later in order to write this. I'm not alone. The film has been remade, and maintains what is always called a cult following, a term which has always puzzled me. One would never say that *Vertigo* or *Touch of Evil*, two other films from the same year which remain popular, have cult followings—they just have followings. The Best Picture Oscar that year went to *Gigi*, a film much more difficult to watch—go on, try sitting through "Thank Heaven for Little Girls"—and yet, instinctively, it feels wrong to say that the better movie is *Attack of the 50 Foot Woman*, which, it bears repeating, is bad.

Seeing this movie, and others like it, I embarked on a period familiar in adolescence, in which rolling one's eyes is much more fun than appreciating something honestly. A prime example would be *Plan 9 from Outer Space*, a famously terrible movie of such staying power that its hypnotically inept writer-director, Ed Wood, is the subject of his own bio pic, something unlikely to happen to countless directors of much better, much less adored films. I saw *Plan 9 from Outer Space* in high school, with a sold-out crowd who recited much of the bonkers dialog ("Future events such as these will affect you in the future") by heart. It remains one of the best cinematic experiences I've had.

It's easy to tag all this as camp, an ironic appreciation for junk culture that, what with the amount of available junk, is endlessly renewable. That would be a familiar narrative, that a fascination for such things is sarcastic, working contrary to the intent of whatever it is you're looking at: The last scene of *Attack of the 50 Foot Woman*, for instance, in which the giantess lies dead clutching the corpse of her philandering husband, the better for the cop to say, "She finally gets Harry all to herself." The only way to enjoy that would be to laugh at it, and laughter is cheap.

But that's all wrong. Camp, as other writers and historians have laid out far more elegantly, is linked to, if not rooted in, queer culture, which found ways to survive, even thrive, in a world hostile to such difference. A sexist film, so misogynist as to seem constructed solely to keep gender in its place, could be celebrated in drag; a shallow pop song about puppy love could instead be a powerful anthem, if you ignore the second verse and look askance at the chorus. Growing up, the word said to indicate this stance was *divine*; sometime in the late eighties it became *fabulous*. It wasn't a way of saying that you liked something bad; it was a way of saying you'd found joy, or perhaps stitched it yourself, from something other people often found ridiculous. *Vertigo* is a great movie. *Attack of the 50 Foot Woman* is fabulous. Both movies turn women into looming fetishes that undo normal men who are, reasonably, we're informed, just trying to completely control the objects of their obsessive interests. In *Vertigo*, a man hires his old college buddy to follow a woman he's hired to pretend to be his wife, the better to have the buddy be a reliable witness for a murder plot involving throwing the already dead wife off a public building. One's joy when viewing *Vertigo* requires accepting this ridiculous plot as not only likely but emotionally engaging, and overlooking the unsavory misogynist undertones. The joy in experiencing *Attack of the 50 Foot Woman* is because of its loopy motives and clumsy execution, demonstrating just how shoddy gendered ideas really are.

But even this isn't really it. Whatever prescriptive value stories like this have, their appeal isn't in whatever counterintuitive lesson you can find or invent in them. As with "The White Snake," these texts have a distinct appeal, tricky to describe but unmistakable to experience. Ed Wood wasn't just a lousy director but a deep outsider, not just queer but incomprehensible, and his movies, especially *Plan 9 from Outer Space*, exude a strange loneliness. One of the notorious details about *Plan 9* is that it contains the final onscreen performance by Bela Lugosi, star of countless monster movies in the 1930s and '40s. By the time Wood found him, Lugosi was crippled by drug addiction, and could only skulk around his yard for a few minutes; the rest of his character's appearances in the film are by another man, who always keeps his face hidden behind a cape in the hopes we won't notice. The effect is a pathetic elegy for a man who played so many monsters he became a mere silent shell; the inept script provides moments of levity in the ill-lit, murky world of Wood's incoherent and doomed vision. Similarly, what is best about *Attack of the 50 Foot Woman* is a few shots toward the end, after she's become 50 feet tall and right before she attacks. We see her walking across the barren California landscape, glowing from radiation, her footsteps echoey booms. It's the simplest visual effect in the movie—a double exposure of a woman walking and some mountains and sky—and the most effective, a genuinely eerie sight of a giantess, angry and free. It's almost identical to what's fascinating about that Baudelaire poem, and many others. It's not that Baudelaire is so bad one has to appreciate him ironically, or that he's a fabulous poet (as opposed to, say, Shakespeare, who is just great.). It's something else. It's crazy. It's not what you're told poetry should be, and the ideas behind its creation are often odious. But they're expressed in a way so contrary to reason, by an artist whose mind is so insensible that his vision, wrong as it is, works.

When I started writing books for children, I know what interested me: Terrible things happening, like in all the best literature. But I wasn't sure it would work—that is, that anyone would agree that this was what children ought to read. The first professional person with whom I shared my idea—terrible things happening over and over to orphaned children—was an editor in a bar at the violet hour, and when she said she liked the idea, I was very embarrassed for her; I thought she couldn't hold her liquor. A few days later, in broad daylight and stone sober, she offered me a contract for four volumes, and I thought at least one of us had gone mad. "Four books?" I said in disbelief to my agent, who reassured me, sensibly, that they'd never publish all four. They published all thirteen volumes, and then many more, but I'm still not sure any of us was wrong.

When *The Bad Beginning* was done, the editor asked what I thought should go on the back of the book, to recommend it to readers. I could not imagine. I walked to a large chain bookstore, squintingly lit, and looked at the backs of all the perky titles children were being offered. Even the good books had smiley sentences on the back, full of exclamation points. I remember looking at the word *zany*, in zany type, and feeling my heart sink. It was not until I stopped at the pharmacy on the way home, and my eyes fell on all the dire warnings on medical packaging, that I realized the Snicket books didn't need exclamation points luring readers toward zaniness. They needed deterrents. Before long, *The Bad Beginning* was published with a pearl-clutching letter from Lemony Snicket on the back, warning readers away: "In this short book alone, the three youngsters encounter a greedy and repulsive villain, itchy clothing, a disastrous fire, a plot to steal their fortune, and cold porridge for breakfast." This packaging has since been described as sarcastic, or, less rudely, reverse psychology, and there's something to that. But just as one can enjoy a bad movie for reasons other than its badness, the Snicket warning isn't sarcastic, as surely as it isn't sincere.

It is in that space, or at least I hope it is, in which the hysteria of the sentences, like the melodramatic tropes of the plot, live in mysterious confluence with whomever might be interested.

This is something I return to when I feel pressured to explain or categorize my work, despite being uniquely unqualified to do so. When I look at anything I've done, all I see is the stitching: the cribbings of things that inspired me, the countless parts I wish I'd done better and a few passages that seem like the best I could have done, and even if unshabby, not quite as good as I'd like. The writers I admire most are, of course, much, much better than I am, and I can't excuse my bouts of ill-fittedness on some deep-set peculiarity—that is, I can't claim to be as bonkers as Ed Wood or Baudelaire. I am, perhaps, more like the Brothers Grimm, who of course did not write "The White Snake" or any other of their tales, but wandered around collecting them so that other people might look them over. I do it now, with "The Giantess," without having much in the way of analysis, only of wonder, and my novels feel the same to me. I send them out into the world for people to see—young people, mostly, usually the best readers—as if telling them a story, or maybe even just some weird premise, which, if they like, they can carry with them. *Last night I dreamed I was a horse.* You don't say. Tell me more.

3

Are you OK?

There's nothing more boring than someone else's dreams. "I had a dream last night," someone will say to you, and no matter how much you desire and admire and respect and treasure them, ten seconds later you will want them to shut up. I had a few more imaginary sentences here, describing some tedious recitation, and I cut them because even a made-up monolog about a dream, made up to show that dreams are boring, is boring.

It could seem a little puzzling, then, that there's so much dreaming in literature. Despite nobody wanting to hear about it, countless novels and poems move into the illogical, too-often italicized world of the narrative unconscious. It could seem puzzling, but it isn't. We know why artists tell us things about their dreams. It's not for us; it's for them. Other people's dreams are boring, but our own, some of them anyway, fascinate us. It is hard to let go of a dream that strikes you. You spend the day shooing it away, laughing at yourself for being unable to quite brush it off like we're supposed to. It is, really, the main difference between the waking world and the life in dreams: The latter is not supposed to matter. Encounter a severed head on your way to work, and you're likely to be excused from the 9:00 a.m. meeting. If you instead begin the meeting talking about a dream you had of beheading, you will just be boring.

The paving over of our dreams finds a parallel in literature, which has, beneath its printed surface, something wild and deranged that's not quite digestible in the culture. An artist will be scrubbed up, through canonization or other forms of visibility, but beneath the widespread presentational version is something too crazy to be truly acceptable. A poet's work contradicts the harmless myths of their life, or vice versa, a novelist's political views suddenly cast their glorious work under inglorious suspicion, an album, a painting, a symphony, a manifesto will fail to conform to some framework we've placed lazily but staunchly across an artist's body of work.

A book I admired recently was *The Emily Dickinson Reader*, poet Paul Legault's translations of Emily Dickinson from English into English—more like summations, actually, of Dickinson's verse into aphorisms. On one hand, the project is something of a joke, reducing iconic American poems to "If you're a flower, I'm kind of like your zombie-gardener" or "God, are you sure you can handle me?" But it's also a reminder of the craziness that's often elided in considerations of Dickinson—and indeed, in all revered literature. It reminds me of something my father, an accountant, told me about a client of his, a psychiatrist, when my father gave some advice on billing clients. "Lou," the psychiatrist said, jokingly and/or with unprofessional candor, "you're forgetting: These people are crazy."

I'm one of those people, with a crazy story that's hard to tell, not at all aided by the glum fact that it begins with a dream I had. I was in my first year in college and living alone in an unshared dorm room. I liked it, except at night, when I was asleep, and some figures would appear in the scraggly tree that waved branches just outside my third floor window. They were people—not people I knew—who were naked and hairless. They were powdery white, terrifying to me, and of course I wanted nothing to do with them. But they made me come with them, out my window, and they showed me something, in a way which reminded me of a painting I'd seen in an American Studies class, *The Artist in His Museum* by the naturalist and inventor Charles Wilson Peale, depicting him lifting a curtain to reveal wondrous exhibits. Behind this curtain were acts of violence. The violence was loud and the figures silent. The victims of the violence were also people I did not know. Sometimes I was participating in this violence—murder and torture with assorted weapons and objects—and sometimes I was just witnessing, or first a witness and then a participant, or even both— you know how slippery such things can be in a dream. And then I'd wake up. I would do all the post-nightmare things—a visit to the echoey coed communal bathroom, a glass of water, some calming breaths by the reassuring glow of the bedstand lamp, maybe a little reading. And then I would go to sleep and it would happen again. It happened every night.

In the morning I would be exhausted and lost, but I was attending a prestigious liberal arts school, so being exhausted and lost did not distinguish me from my classmates, and for a while I don't think anyone, including myself, found much amiss. How could something be wrong, really? Dreams—surely that's what they were—are not important, and although I'd always been a healthy sleeper, I was also suspicious of sleep.

When I was eight, my mother, who is still apologizing for this, took me to see the remake of *Invasion of the Body Snatchers*, in which the pod people get you if you fall asleep. (It also contains, and I do not say this lightly, Jeff Goldblum's greatest performance.) This was, of course, terrifying to me as a child, but the film also made me look askance at the eerie, omnipresent phenomenon of sleeping, which, properly considered, was easily as spooky as the movie's plot. In eighth grade I wrote a school report on sleep, using as source material a fascinating book called *Some Must Watch While Some Must Sleep*, by William C. Dement, who for some reason autographed ("to Dan") the copy I still have. In it is an anecdote which fascinated me and made me very envious:

> Professor Morgan told us that it had been his custom to sleep six to eight hours each night until he went to Germany on a fellowship at the age of twenty-three. The change in his sleep habits occurred with unexplained suddenness. One night he went to bed at his usual time of ten o'clock, but woke up at two and could not go back to sleep. He thought little of it, until the next night when, in spite of the same ten o'clock bedtime, he again wakened at two. This time, out of sheer boredom, he lit his candle, and resumed the studies he had discontinued at bedtime.

This four-hour sleep pattern continued for the rest of his life—and the professor was quite pleased about it. It did not make him sleepy during the day, and it enabled him to be enormously productive in his academic life. In his retirement years, he continued to waken early, and often stayed in bed passing the time in some useful pursuit such as knitting. He commented that nearly every one of his many friends owned at least one afghan that had been produced entirely before sunrise.

How I envied Professor Morgan and his secret candlelit life. I still daydream—not knitting—about what I would do with those extra hours while everyone else is sleeping. In my actual life, however, the figures kept appearing, every night in my room. They were not just disturbing me but were beginning to disturb other people—people who crashed on my floor, or, occasionally, shared my bed. I started to hear what I've always thought is a very beautiful sentence, both comforting and extremely sad, that simultaneously reminds us of how all people are connected and how isolated, also, each of us is from everybody else. It's a sentence I say all the time, of course, given the world, and one I leave unspoken even more often, in places—airports, lobbies— where strangers are waiting together, or at red lights, with people I don't know idling next to me in their cars: *Are you OK?*

Of course I was. People had bad dreams all the time. At dusk, though, I began to have a feeling, prickly and heavy, along my shoulders and at the shivering tips of my fingers. It's a feeling difficult to describe without alluding to B movies and gothic thrillers: the steely and fearsome certainty that something dreadful will happen when the sun goes down, the haunting imagery of a recurring dream, the clouds parting to a full moon and the long night ahead. It was nowhere near as romantic as it was on paper, though there was something, too, about turning pages in a book, that reminded me of how the dreams felt, if indeed they were dreams at all. They didn't feel like dreams, I began to admit.

"What do they feel like?" a friend asked me.

"Like when I go to sleep," I said, "my whole life is on paper, but cheap paper—a newspaper or a magazine—and then it's ripped away, by these figures I'm seeing, to show me what's underneath," and my friend suggested gently that I take a walk with her over to the mental health center.

I didn't mind therapy—I like to talk—but no matter how much I dug into things that had happened to me, all when I was awake, over the years, I did not improve. I was getting so little sleep that the daylight hours had an unsettling hue, a slight haze or filter that made reality seem that much more fraught and fragile. No Professor Morgan, I. I was missing classes, getting clumsy and forgetful, an unreliable friend, a disastrous boyfriend. Something else began happening, too. No one knew what to call it: fainting, seizuring, dropping. My exhausted brain would just fall from its bearings, like bicycle chains do; my mind would spin, faster and faster, and I'd fall twitching to the floor. One of these spells happened at the top of a flight of stairs, at the house of my girlfriend's family. I was holding a box of something that clattered to the ground, I can't remember what, but when I awoke, it was everywhere, and my girlfriend's father, a doctor but not the kind who could help me, said, in a mix of kindness and concern for the person his daughter was getting involved with, that whatever was happening to me, I needed to fix it, or something terrible was going to happen.

I was referred to an array of experts in a widening circle around the campus, in a variety of office settings, none comforting. I spent a night with electrodes all over my head and shoulders, like tinsel, in a crummy building that felt like it held the last of true believers in something doubtful, cryptozoologists or trackers of UFOs, waiting for the times to catch up with them or, more likely, leave them behind. I went to a storefront office in a minimall and was evaluated to the tune of inkblots and lengthy questionnaires. I was blindfolded and told to fit an assortment of wooden blocks into some kind of framework, and then the framework was overturned and I was told to do it again, a task so senseless and disorienting that I began to cry. There is, of course, nothing that makes you feel crazier than being tested to see how crazy you are. I kept thinking, faintly but persistently, the same thing everyone thinks: That there must be some mistake. After all, these were just dreams that were happening. Dreams were boring; nobody wants to hear about dreams. They were not, could not be, important.

But of course, as in a B movie, what starts with bad dreams doesn't just putter out, and one afternoon I was walking across campus. It had been a year or so of these terrible things happening, and across the deep green lawn of the beautiful campus I saw, at some distance, one of the figures that had been appearing to me at night, naked, bald, painted or powdered white. For a moment I thought someone was fucking with me. Swiveling around I could see that none of the other people on the lawn

41

could see what I was seeing. The figure looked right at me, as blank as usual. I knew what would happen, frightened as I was, when my mind started to race like it was, and I managed to be on the grass when I fell unconscious. I was very, very frightened, but not just because I was hallucinating—surely that's what it was—but because I realized, there on the lawn, that what was happening was not an aberration, some blip I'd leave behind. I wasn't having bad dreams, or a troublesome year. It was instead the road I was on. I was stuck with it. I fell knowing that this was something that would stay with me for the rest of my days. I've had the feeling since—realizing I'd found the love of my life, or that my infant son was my permanent responsibility. I realized it outside an auditorium in a city where I knew no one, with a long line of strangers waiting under a marquee reading LEMONY SNICKET, and I began to see that this name would stay with me forever. But right then I was feeling it about these visitors, these figments on the lawn.

It's hard to remember how things progressed, as it was hard to keep track of it then. I kept having seizures; I kept seeing things. Various plans, various drugs, failed. Somehow I learned that the figures I was seeing were similar to those of Butoh dancers, practitioners of a Japanese art, and I wrote to a troupe in Japan—what they must have thought—and never heard back. I painted myself white, with white shoe polish in my hair, and was photographed for my girlfriend's art project, which had no discernible effect; I pursued more bad ideas that I didn't tell anyone about, and more, I'm sure, that even I don't know anymore. I just kept getting worse, and with mental health, getting worse means *getting worse*. I was becoming a worse person, skittish, mercurial, desperate, nobody you'd want to know. I maintained best I could, but what was there to maintain, really, with figures from violent dreams appearing in doorways, on street corners, sometimes in groups, far away or so close by I had to walk right through them? With reality like this, about what was there really to keep an even keel?

Then in the middle of a paper I was writing, about the colonialist implications in H. G. Wells's *Empire of the Ants*, I had a seizure, the biggest yet. When I woke up I could not read or write or speak. My housemate called an ambulance. We were renting a place with a few other friends, on a residential block, and I remember the worried faces of the neighbors—not other students but grown adults—as I was sirened away, wondering if I was OK.

Nobody wants to be a medical mystery. Doctors get excited, briefly, but when a pet theory and its new examinations don't pan out, they get tired of making wilder and wilder guesses. My brain was rescanned, awake and asleep, and my parents flew in to listen to arguments about anomalies and what they might mean. Studies of my sleep patterns revealed that, when having these experiences, I was not quite asleep, or maybe I was, or they didn't know. Speech returned gradually, over a period of days, but reading and writing were lost for months, months in which the world, unreadable to me, was even more discombobulating and frightening than it was already. Simple signs, or titles on TV, looked like they came from an alphabet so foreign I could not even say how many words were in front of me. I could scarcely copy shapes onto a piece of paper, and books people brought me when they visited, always a reliable source of solace, were an alien reminder that I had become detached from a large swath of ordinary life. Looking at language began to feel like looking at a skull, maybe my own. I was referred elsewhere, consulted thoroughly, released to the care of very worried people, usually me. I was hypnotized repeatedly—you can find me in a book by the hypnotist—and a doctor used the word "schizophrenia" out loud, causing my mother to leave the room. In the hospital, I was afraid to sleep, and they were afraid to make me. I stayed up late, staring at the phone number at the bottom of the screen during advertisements for psychics who used their powers to sort you out. I was tempted to call, but I couldn't read the numbers.

This is when something happened—something I remember, if remember is the word. I cannot be sure it happened. Some doctors have told me it's a standard procedure; others have said no way, you must be kidding. One doctor gave me both answers, on each of the two separate occasions when I asked him if it could be true.

What I remember is sitting in a chair while two women, nurses or technicians, took a small simple tool, almost a can opener, and poked two small slits in my arm, the smooth side, between my elbow and my wrist. Then they sat and let me bleed. They had a stack of index cards, which they ripped in half, and when it seemed like my blood was clotting—if clotting is what I mean—which they determined by twisting my arm one way or another, they scraped off the hardening blood with one of the torn cards, reddening the edge. While this went on, they had a conversation with each other: One of the women was dating a preacher and was trying to figure out if she was cut out to be a preacher's wife, and the other one was listening sympathetically and telling her to follow her heart. I thought about my own heart, pumping out blood, and then they were done, and counted the blood-tipped cards, writing the total down on a scrap of paper. Could this have happened? Were they measuring something with my blood flow? Is there some part of the procedure—a timer? a drug I'd been given?—that I'm not remembering that renders this more sensible? The time I spent in the hospital was so confusing and scary that I'm tempted to think it didn't happen at all, but I have two tiny scars on my arm, right where I remember it. They're hardly visible, especially after so much time—certainly not noticeable enough that anyone asks about them, but sometimes when I tell someone the story, they lean in close, to see the little marks.

In any case, everyone gave up. A doctor came, sat on my bed, and said, "I don't know, what do you think it is?" Perhaps this was meant to be comforting, for my opinion to be taken seriously, or perhaps it was some plan to build esprit de corps, to entertain the notion that we were all in this together. In any case, it made me cry. I felt as if a firefighter, having arrived at my blazing house, was asking me what I thought they ought to do. But I told him. I had, after all, been thinking about it for a long time. Heaving with sobs, I told him that maybe the reason they couldn't find the cause of my hallucinations or my dreams is that I wasn't hallucinating or dreaming. Maybe the figures I saw were real. I did not know what they were exactly—ghosts, aliens, whatever other word we could dream up—but they were not a medical phenomenon. They were an actual thing, actually happening.

If you say such things, there are only two places you end up. My family had health insurance and money, so in my case, I didn't end up on the streets. Instead I arrived at a place not entirely unlike a dorm, except that orientation meant they took my belt and my shoes. At intake they read to me the exact same questionnaire I'd been given, over the years, over and over again; I remember one question was whether or not I could repeat the phrase "no ifs, ands or buts." I had so memorized the list of questions that I uttered the phrase before the woman had a chance to prompt me.

"No ifs, ands or buts," I said to her.

She was startled.

"I'm psychic," I deadpanned, and she liked this. She wrote something down in a bonus blank and gave me a professional smile.

"Do you think you know what I'm thinking now?" she asked, and I realized, even in my desolate state, that deadpan humor was not the coping mechanism to reach for just then. The thing was, though, that I did know what she was thinking. She was thinking I was a crazy person, and I was thinking it, too. I knew that my explanation for what was happening must be a sign of craziness, because it was both very sensible to me and bonkers on its face, and besides, I seemed to be in a place where crazy people ended up. *When in Rome*, I thought.

There were something like twelve people in the place, lying around a few sex-segregated rooms and walking the clean, smelly hallways. For the first couple of nights I slept in a gurney by the nurses' station, so my nightmares wouldn't disturb the other residents. In the morning, we'd take turns in the bathrooms, where we were not allowed to have sex. Before they let me have a razor to shave with, they asked me if I felt safe. I remember, behind the person asking me, a staring figure no one else could see.

In the afternoons, nothing happened. People took turns going into offices for therapy, so I must have had a turn, but I can't remember anything about that at all. Mostly we sat. About half the people were women with eating disorders, who would each carry around an apple and a paper cup, so they could taste the fruit and spit it out. The next largest group were skinny, well-manicured young men from religious families—an equal split between Catholic and Muslim—who had attempted suicide. Their issue seemed transparently obvious to me, and puzzling that it went unmentioned, until I met the head honcho, a quiet tyrannical man from central casting, who referred to these young men as "confused." I had a Keith Haring T-shirt, standard issue at my school, so the young men came to me. I was in a very fragile state but did my best, explaining to them, fuck that doctor, there is no God, or if there is He doesn't care who you love, and that in my experience the best way to figure out if you really like guys is the same as figuring out if you like Korean food: Try some.

There was a last group, more diverse in appearance and behavior but also of a piece. There was a boy in high school who had witnessed his father kill his mother and who was, in the staff parlance, acting out. There was a quiet meth casualty. There was a woman so frightened and angry, who refused to change her clothes, that you hated to hear the story, not that she would tell it to you. There was a normal-enough looking guy suffering from burns, horrendous burns from a fire, which no one but he could see and feel. This was the group I was in, the group most like me. When I think of them now, that same question comes to me, *Are you OK?*, and I hope they all are. It was not a question asked of them much there, as far as I could tell. They were not—*we* were not—people about whom anyone knew what to do. I was given, for instance, a dose of sodium pentothal—truth serum, basically, prompting me to recite a few lines from *Goldfinger* ("No, Mr. Bond, I expect you to die") as it was administered. I cannot imagine what they hoped I would say—some forgotten trauma, perhaps—but I felt as if a great weight had been lifted, and spoke joyously and at length about the homophobia I saw amongst the staff, tracing it to their own Victorian fear of sex and their own bodies—I had, after all, read two volumes of Foucault's *History of Sexuality*—and that if only we could all be honest about the nature of desire, there would hardly be a need for places like this, but that as the system stood now there was no cultural incentive to help people in such a way that would make this corrupt institution unnecessary, and they put me to bed.

Occasionally we got to take supervised walks, blinking in the sunshine in a one or two block radius. There someone called my name, a middle-aged woman with a stack of papers stacked on the hood of her beat-up car. I recognized her at once. It was my Nabokov professor.

It's a little tricky to describe how much the work of Vladimir Nabokov meant to me at the time, but if there was anything else that gave me the feeling that something was to have an enormous and permanent effect on my psyche, besides pale figures from violent nightmares, it would be the prose of this glorious American author. I'd read *Lolita* before college, and found it far more difficult and depressing than the sexual romp its cultural notoriety had promised me, so I'm not sure what prompted me to take an entire class on his work. But when I did, I fell hard. His sentences rolled around in my mind, multi-tentacled with loopy vocabulary, inscrutable jokes and fierce opinions, sentences that stayed luminous whether you picked them apart like a scholar or just gobbled them up. The more I read, the more enormous his work felt in my head. I liked how his plots approached genres like melodrama or mystery and yet remained independent and unpredictable. I liked how his books had the gossamer effect of escapism and yet remained in the real world's gravitational pull—in fact, the world felt more magic, more elaborate in detail and experience, just taking a walk or looking at ordinary items, after spending time reading him.

It was this last phenomena, how something can be fanciful and realistic at the same time, which mesmerized me most, the way it recreated the very experience of reading, of your mind being led someplace else even as you know where you really are. Nabokov famously said that reality was "one of the few words which mean nothing without quotes," and this was an idea that kept visiting, bringing me comfort and bliss at a time when my mind was desperate for both.

The professor and I only had a brief conversation, there on the street, and it was not about Nabokov. I think she was both surprised and not surprised to see me where I was. She'd watched me deteriorate over the past years, even as she advised me on a thesis comparing Nabokov's performative reality to that of the Marx Brothers, my mind trying to sharpen and hone a specific, maybe absurd little rhetorical point while so much around me shattered. But I think to see me in such crazy company seemed wrong. Later, she told me that she'd had the idea to whisk me away in her car, which seems like the premise for a Nabokovian plot. She did not say anything like that then, of course, and I can't say I had some Nabokovian epiphany talking to her. But sometime after they led me back, something changed in how I was.

One of my favorite Nabokov novels is a relatively obscure one, *Invitation to a Beheading*, which could almost pass for Kafka if you squint. Its clumsy hero, Cincinnatus C., finds himself in a prison both ridiculous and frightening, clearly imaginary and yet hopelessly restrictive to his person. Condemned to death, he arrives at the platform and, after the executioner tells him to count to ten, there arrives one of my favorite passages in all of literature:

> One Cincinnatus was counting, but the other Cincinnatus had already stopped heeding the sound of the unnecessary count which was fading away in the distance; and, with a clarity he had never experienced before—at first almost painful, so suddenly did it come, but then suffusing him with joy, he reflected: why am I here? Why am I lying like this? And, having asked himself these simple questions, he answered them by getting up and looking around.
>
> All around there was a strange confusion. Through the headsman's still swinging hips the railing showed. On

the steps the pale librarian sat doubled up, vomiting. The spectators were quite transparent, and quite useless, and they all kept surging and moving away—only the back rows, being painted rows, remained in place. Cincinnatus slowly descended from the platform and walked off through the shifting debris. He was overtaken by Roman, who was now many times smaller and who was at the same time Rodrig: "What are you doing!" he croaked, jumping up and down. "You can't, you can't! It's dishonest toward him, toward everybody . . . Come back, lie down—after all, you were lying down, everything was ready, everything was finished!" Cincinnatus brushed him aside and, he, with a bleak cry, ran off, already thinking only of his own safety.

Little was left of the square. The platform had long since collapsed in a cloud of reddish dust. The last to rush past was a woman in a black shawl, carrying the tiny executioner like a larva in her arms. The fallen trees lay flat and reliefless, while those that were still standing, also two-dimensional, with a lateral shading of the trunk to suggest roundness, barely held on with their branches to the ripping mesh of the sky. Everything was coming apart. Everything was falling. A spinning wind was picking up and whirling: dust, rags, chips of painted wood, bits of gilded plaster, pasteboard bricks, posters; an arid gloom fleeted; and amidst the dust, and the falling things, and the flapping scenery, Cincinnatus made his way in that direction where, to judge by the voices, stood beings akin to him.

One I reason I love this passage is that it is beautiful. Another is that it saved my life. "Inspiration" is too meager a description for what these words did, but there in the psychiatric ward I remembered them and lived by their principles. The bungling hero of a novel I loved manages to think his way out of something from there appears to be no escape; I, too, was a bungler—I literally could not stop falling down—but to some extent, I knew I was also in a prison of my own making, and I was not interested in being imprisoned any longer. I began, there in my hopeless and helpless state, to give different answers to the questions being put to me. Having deduced lines to say out loud that would let me out, I let myself out of where I was. I told the doctors, as professionally as I could, that they were not helping me. It felt like a breakup; I thought we both should see other people. I stopped taking drugs—drugs which, I feel obliged to add, work wonders for many, many people. There was a reality—or, more properly, a "reality"—in which I could continue to fall, but not to spend time in the wretched circumstances in which I had found myself. The goal was not to stop terrible things from happening—all around me, terrible things kept happening to me, to my fellow patients, and to everyone walking the streets—but to somehow make them presentable enough to be allowed to leave. I did not stop seeing things. I changed the way I talked about them. They were certainly not real. Only a lunatic would think that. They were hallucinations, of course they were, and I was going to live with them, not in a hospital, where they would be a constant occupation, but in the world, in "reality," in which they are not talked about, or you are taken away.

I would hate to have anyone infer that I was "cured" by a passage in a novel that I took to heart, or to believe even for a moment (because I do not) that mental health is largely a question of attitude. I still, to this day, see these figures, frequently but not frighteningly, not anymore. Nobody else has ever said they see them, too. My seizures—surely, that's what they are—are few and far between, but over the years I've more or less pinpointed their cause, never suggested to me in years of medical attention, which is prosaically obvious: I get them when I don't get enough sleep. When they occur now, I am usually jetlagged, or have had sleep stolen from me, for whatever reason, several nights in a row. I've learned when to keep an ear to the ground, and how to hear them coming. And I've learned to look away, to keep walking, to move through the figures I see, as if they are inappropriate, just staring strangers, not worth mentioning. Indeed, to the bafflement of people who've known me all this time, I hardly mention them, and all this will be news to many friends I have now. I'm not a crazy person, not because "crazy" is inaccurate but because it is redundant, unspeakable, and invisible. If I were a crazy person, babbling about visitations from ghostly figures, I would not be allowed to run around loose. If I just had bad dreams sometimes, the thing was not to talk about them; everybody had them, and talking about your dreams is boring.

When I think of this journey and the choices it led me to, in which the haziness of "reality" managed to save me from the terrible things that were going on, I think of a place I traveled to, to talk about my work. My way was paid, and a fee negotiated, and I was put up, not in a miserable psychiatric ward but in the swankiest place they could find, a hotel with a vast lobby with a body of water, a lake or pond you could call it, fed by a waterfall and surrounded by little bridges and lanterns and plants and trees, all under a tall domed atrium. A free man, grateful and thirsty, hard at work in my waking life, I sat and had a drink at the bar, and noticed a tall tree—which seemed impossible even with such a sumptuous decorating plan—hanging over the barman, and I asked him if it was real.

"No, no," he said, and knocked on the plastic trunk. "It's fake. But the waterfall's real."

I stood up. I looked around. I knew just what he meant.

4

Wrong.

The wrong-headed notions of childhood are so often so preferable to life on Earth. When my son was very young, he conflated, understandably, the kind of ticket you need for entrance to some cultural event or institution with the citation kind. Until I cruelly set him right, he lived in an inviting world in which motorists who parked in a fire zone were kindly given a slip of paper gaining them entrance to the zoo, instead of the real, dismal world of thoughtless action and bureaucratic scolding. It's something I love to think about, how little we know, how wrong we are about so much when we are new to the world.

When I was young, I would go with my father to the library, a walk after dinner once a week or so. He would smoke a cigar and talk about things, and I would half-listen, as one does in childhood, see-sawing slowly in and out of participation in the tangible world. When we got to the library, my father would leave me in the children's room and go to find thrillers or histories of the Holocaust, which he had escaped when he was about the age I was then. Eric Ambler was a favorite author of his, and I remember the name of the author, and how we went to find him, blurred in my head, *Ambler, ambling* to the library.

I had very good librarians in the children's room. Like my father's words on the way, they're a blur in my head, but I know they took me seriously and put many, many crucial books in my hands. I remember a book I wish I could find now—a book for children about Malcolm X, when I was at an age when the last name "X" was so intriguing that it was reason enough to read about him. The book made him seem not just brave and passionate but sensible, so by the time I encountered him in a history class, where textbooks tended to shade him with white worry, I knew he was right. Mostly, though, I read fiction. A favorite author was Zilpha Keatley Snyder, whose books explore issues of class and race under the guise of stories of the supernatural. Best known, then and now, for *The Egypt Game*, I preferred *The Changeling*, about a timid girl from a privileged family who befriends a girl from one considered "fallen" and "troubled." Their friendship is deemed so ill-fitting by those around them that one day the girls decide, while climbing trees, that one of them is a changeling—a mythological or supernatural creature switched out at birth and raised, incorrectly, as an ordinary human:

> "Aunt Evaline and I think I might be a wood nymph or a water sprite or something like that. See, when I was born and my mother was so sick afterwards, with all those other kids and everything, nobody paid much attention to me at all, until I went to live with Aunt Evaline. And

by then it was already too late. I suppose that was why I liked it so much right away at Aunt Evaline's. I didn't really belong where I was before, so no wonder I like it better with her."

While Ivy was talking, she had finished tieing the last knot; and then sliding her legs over and down the dangling rope, she slid off the limb. She slid slowly down the twisting rope, approaching Martha's level and then dropping below it, so that her face spun in and out of sight. Watching Ivy floating, spinning downward, in and out of sunlight, no one could have doubted for a moment.

"Of course," Martha said to herself, "a changeling. That explains everything."

But by the time she had reached the ground, climbing slowly and carefully, feeling cautiously for the very safest handholds, Martha had decided to ask just one more question.

"Do *you* really believe it?" she asked. "About changelings and everything."

"I believe in just about everything," Ivy said.

That beautiful declaration, which ends a chapter—"I believe in just about everything"—is a daring idea, unfashionable then and now, that imagination is the way to best solve our most vexing issues. As a child reading it, all I got were goosebumps. There is plenty to admire in this passage—the tucked-in details of Ivy's autobiography, the two tree-climbing techniques setting up what is opposite about the girls as they strive for common ground—but I think it was likely the cadences of Snyder's language that I found mesmerizing. The lulling, slightly off repetition in the descriptions ("down the dangling rope/down the twisting rope," "in and out of sight/in and out of sunlight") match my own spacy consciousness at that age, and I read *The Changeling* over and over, a little sad that my obvious physical resemblances to my family meant it was very unlikely I was a changeling myself, and I read all of her books my library had, and ones they fetched from other branches, until one week there were none I hadn't devoured. The following week, there still wasn't a new one, but I was prepared to give Zilpha Keatley Snyder a break—perhaps she was on vacation. By the third week I was annoyed—how long could such a thing take?—and one of these blurry librarians explained, to my astonishment, that it took a long time to write and publish a book. Years later this would haunt me, when thousands of children, in bookstore lines and in countless letters, asked me when a new Snicket volume would be available, the latest volume being out for some weeks. I knew exactly what they meant, and couldn't help feeling that they were right, that I, for the umpteenth time, was wrong.

By the time I was reading *The Changeling* I had wanted to be a writer for some time. My parents used to tell a story that when I was six, when asked what I wanted to be when I grew up, I said, an old man who lives at the top of the mountain giving people advice. If this story is true—and I have my doubts—then that is the only other career I have ever seriously considered, and by the time I was wondering why Zilpha Keatley Snyder was so lazy, I was beginning to notice the way literature was made—that is, not just the story but the way the sentences knocked around. I got very, very interested in this passage in a book by Ellen

Conford, *And This Is Laura*, in which our heroine sits down to breakfast with her family, including her brother Dennis, who likes to recite television commercials he's memorized:

It is a drizzly morning in late September as we look in on the Hoffman household. A typical Monday at 522 Woodbine Way, with nothing to distinguish it from any other Monday. As we join the Hoffmans, we hear Laura say . . .

"But that's not logical. If you're so concerned with our individual likes and dislikes at breakfast, how come we all have to eat the same thing for dinner?"

"Because preparing dinner is more trouble than preparing breakfast. Therefore, preparing six dinners would be six times more difficult than preparing five breakfasts."

"That's logical," my father said.

"And besides," my mother went on, "anyone who doesn't like what we have for dinner is always free to go and cook whatever he or she prefers."

"What's the matter, Joe? You're so grumpy today. Frankly, Bill, this irregularity is getting me down. I've tried everything—"

"Dennis, *please*. Not first thing in the morning." Jill held her hand to her head.

"Nagging headache? Why suffer? For fast, fast, fast relief—"

"DENNIS!"

"Douglas, dear, I think your pizza is burning."

He didn't look up from his newspaper. " 'S all right. I like it that way."

"It's not enough," I said irritably, "that he has to eat pizza for breakfast—it's got to be burnt pizza."

Douglas sighed and plopped his paper down on the table. "All right, all right, Fussbudget. I'll take it out so it doesn't offend your delicate sense of smell."

"Don't do it on my account," I snapped. "I was just worried about your being able to read the paper through all that black smoke."

"You're exaggerating slightly." He snatched the pizzas out of the oven and dropped them onto a plate. "As usual."

Douglas is sixteen. He's extremely sarcastic. I don't exaggerate. I report everything *exactly* as it happens.

I read this over and over. I liked—I *still* like—the whole pace of this passage. The mock-theatrical opening ("As we join the Hoffmans . . .") and then the parental argument, with a veneer of wit and charm that, even then, I knew wasn't realistic but aspirational—a charming Noël Cowardly banter so many of us fantasize we maintain as we stutter and stammer our way through actual talking—punctuated by Dennis's recitations, uncited but understood, that toggle our attention a little. It was that last paragraph that ran around my head the most. After a few long-winded sentences—"I was just worried about your being able to read the paper through all that black smoke," "He snatched the pizzas out of the oven and dropped them on a plate"—there's the comparative rat-a-tat of short declaratives: "Douglas is sixteen. He's extremely sarcastic. I don't exaggerate."—and then that sharp and lovely "I report everything *exactly* as it happens," that italicized *exactly* after so much theatrical invention. If I were romanticizing, I would say that I copied this passage out, or took a lot of notes in the margins. I didn't. It was just another thing I held in my head. I wanted to write—not like that, really, but with that instinct or expertise, finding the right rhythm for whatever it was I wanted to say.

Clearly I was ready to read books for grownups, and I have a memory, possibly imaginary, of a librarian leading me grandly out of the children's section into the magnificent ballroom of the main reading room of the West Portal Branch of the San Francisco Library, a glorious aerial shot centered around my wide-eyed joy. In reality I probably just went there some day. I still ambled with my father to the library sometimes, but I more often went by myself, after school or in other empty spaces. I liked being alone and unsupervised, in a quiet place. No one helped me, and I didn't need help. I encountered so much literature this way, without any guidance or context. I had a vague plan of moving through the fiction section backward, starting at Z, and so an early find was *Fish Preferred*, a novel by P. G. Wodehouse. The edition was a common sort at the library—a hardcover, no dustjacket, a simple geometric design stamped on the cover, and no more information than the title and the author's last name. I found the title interesting—more than the publishers did, apparently, as it was later changed to *Summer Lightning*—so I took it home, and when I started it I found it ridiculous:

> Blandings Castle slept in the sunshine. Dancing little
> ripples of heat-mist played across its smooth lawns and
> stone-flagged terraces. The air was full of the lulling drone

of insects. It was that gracious hour of a summer afternoon, midway between luncheon and tea, when Nature seems to unbutton its waistcoat and put its feet up.

The word *twee* was not yet in my vocabulary, but this was too twee for me. My primary exposure to British culture was through Monty Python—as some readers of *The Reptile Room*, with a herpetologist named Uncle Monty, have surmised—but this wasn't sketch comedy. This was a novel, a serious novel—just look at the stark geometric on the cover—and I found this too overwritten to be taken seriously. "Dancing little ripples!" "Midway between luncheon and tea!" "Waistcoat!" The whole thing was ridiculous.

In the shade of a laurel bush outside the back premises of this stately home of England, Beach, butler to Clarence—

Beach?

ninth Earl of Emsworth, its proprietor, sat sipping the contents of a long glass—

I had no idea what a long glass was, but the phrase, then and now, is intriguing, to a non-Brit anyway, in its deceptive simplicity.

—and reading a weekly paper devoted to the doings of Society and the Stage. His attention had just been arrested by a photograph in an oval border on one of the inner pages: and perhaps for a minute he scrutinized this in a slow, thorough, pop-eyed way, absorbing its every detail. Then, with a fruity chuckle, he took a penknife from his pocket, cut out the photograph, and placed it in the recesses of his costume.

At this point—or, more accurately, at "fruity chuckle," which, to a bookish twelve-year-old, had the familiar tang of so much homophobic taunting—I was ready to give up. One thing about writing for children is that they are generally unpersuaded to stick with a book they do not like straightaway. Most of us in later life are willing to give a book at least a few pages, especially if there are indications, such as a friend's recommendation or a Pulitzer Prize, that it's worth our time. Young readers have much less patience for such nonsense. But then the next lines—

At this moment, the laurel bush, which had hitherto not spoken, said "Psst!"

The butler started violently. A spasm ran through his ample frame.

"Beach!" said the bush.

—made me realize, with as much relief as happiness, that this was *supposed to be ridiculous*. Dizzy and dizzyingly, I read on. I had been wrong, and I kept being wrong.

I assumed that *Will You Please Be Quiet, Please?* would be a funny book, which made Raymond Carver's melancholy all the more startling; I tried *The Pillow Book* because it had an alluring cover, and the phrase "pillow talk" was in my head somehow, so I assumed it would have a lot of sex, which made its exploration of gender all the more fraught. I read Ralph Ellison's *Invisible Man* all the way through, generally bewildered and specifically confused as to why it had so little resemblance to the spooky old Universal monster movie I had seen. I read Thomas Thompson's lurid and sleazy novel *Celebrity*, all 561 pages of it, and I remember asking my mother, who must have been suppressing laughter, about whether or not its length made the book *an epic*, a category that somehow seemed important to me, and hearing that no, it doesn't count as an epic if it's written really terribly, a conclusion I still find unconvincing. I read without regard to reputation or cultural stamp, knowing nothing, *caring* nothing, for any of the subtle hierarchies by which pedants try to regulate art. Another way of saying this is that I was wrong all the time. I had no knowledge of these subtle hierarchies because I had no real grasp yet of the word *subtle*. I had a word in my head, *suttle*, which I'd heard aloud, and I'd read the word *subtle*, which I understood to have a similar meaning. Moreover, I understood that saying "subtle" out loud, pronouncing the *b* because of course that's how it was pronounced, always got a laugh, but I didn't know why. It was not until high school, when someone read out loud from a book, that the two words clicked together, like the dual images of a 3D movie, into one.

There's a strange vertigo when you realize you're wrong about something. You float in space for a moment, the landscape seesawing or vanishing into the distance. It's the same feeling when you're completely immersed in a good book and then, at the conclusion of a chapter or the intrusion of a noise, blink your way back to real life. You were wrong about the world, wrong about where you were. You weren't in the world of the book. You were here. It's a powerful feeling and I think an important one, being wrong. People talk about epiphanies, often forgetting that a moment where something clicks into place—where you think you've figured something out—is also a moment where you realized you were wrong about something before. Very wrong, perhaps, or even blissfully wrong. This all has a negative connotation to it—due in part, I think, to the tolling sound the word makes, *wrong wrong wrong*—but there's a certain kind of pleasure that comes with this vertigo. The discord that arises from leaning, incorrectly, on some idea that collapses under you carries with it a small thrill, if not of progress, then at least of travel.

A quartet of books I wrote for children, titled collectively *All the Wrong Questions*, plays with the idea that the journey of a noir detective is akin to the journey of childhood, because of this regular tolling of being wrong. Young Lemony Snicket attempts to solve a twisty mystery that grows more and more enormous and out of his grasp. Everything he thinks he can rely on—friends, responsible adults, the law, the library—are things about which he turns out to be wrong. "I had been wrong over and over and over again," he says, at the conclusion of the first volume, "wrong every time about every clue to the dark and inky mystery hanging over me and everybody else. It rang like a bell in my head—wrong, wrong, wrong. I was wrong, I thought, but maybe if I stayed in this town long enough, I could make everything right." To me, it is the essence of mystery, being wrong— the essence of storytelling, even, as all stories, as they reveal details in the order most enticing to the reader, are mysteries. And life's a mystery, of course, which is why all of us, like Lemony Snicket, are so wrong all the time.

For instance, Ingrid Bergman and Ingmar Bergman are not the same person. It's understandable—*forgivable*, is what's often said, as if the Bergmans need to forgive me for believing this false truth for many years, in some stumble of reading or pronunciation akin to "subtle" and "suttle." Plenty of people make this very mistake—there is even a reminder at the tops of both Bergman pages in an online encyclopedia—but over the years I embroidered this wrong belief with a narrative about which I grew not only more certain but more passionate, a narrative in no way supported by anything anyone could have told me or anything I might have read. The narrative was that Ingrid Bergman, the beautiful cinematic starlet, gradually aged and became less marketable by the sexist Hollywood system, and so returned to her native Sweden, where she became the most innovative film director of her time. And nobody talked about the fact that she was a woman! That she'd honed her skills playing trembling beauties in genre films, only to explode those boundaries once she came into her own! And in that era! Think of all that women were denied in the world of film, and somehow Bergman managed, through ingenuity and grit, to achieve not one but two careers, back to back, and leave behind as legacy (along with Isabella Rossellini), an unfettered artistic vision of gorgeous integrity!

I was in college when a professor in a film seminar—I, believing all these things, was allowed into a *film seminar*—uttered the words "Ingmar Bergman, not to be confused with Ingrid Bergman," and as the room bubbled with knowing chuckles, I made a mental note to check up on something later, and then, after just a few seconds, realized there was nothing to check up on.

Of course they were different people. *Of course* the entire story I had in my head was wrong. I bring this up not to illustrate that I made a fairly common mistake, but that my mind was so eager to make hay with things I was supposedly concerned with—film, art-making, balancing creative impulse with the demands of the capitalist juggernaut, the gender inequalities which give rise to inspiring feminist action—and I wish I could tell you this was an isolated incident.

I know I am not alone in this. You are with me. We are the same audience, let's say, in a darkened theater, staring at the world as if it is projected on a screen, and believing things which aren't true. I can say this with complete confidence, because of the small group of people whom I know for certain will read this book, two of them were with me, not long ago, in the Castro Theatre in San Francisco, watching a film by Jean-Luc Godard. After about an hour of the more or less straightforward film, there was a prolonged shot of an upside-down room, and then soundtracked by some gurgly noises, the figure of a person walking on the ceiling. All of us—me, my wife, a dear friend, and the rest of the audience—sat and considered this strange but not unenjoyable choice. And then, after a few minutes, the light dawned: we realized that the second reel of the film had been inserted incorrectly into the projector. And even that phrase, *the light dawned,* calls to mind an enormous way in which we've been wrong. It seems to be every fiction writer and poet's favorite bit of science, recited so frequently and enthusiastically like a first grader telling you a spider isn't an insect. Light, according to physicists, behaves sometimes like a particle and sometimes like a wave, and so is somehow both, or one sometimes and the other the other. To make sure I had this right, I read a slim volume on physics, the sort of book published for us creative types and the sort I've read a few times before, without quite gasping much past the fact that we're wrong about light. Very wrong. It's not a wave and it's not a particle; it's something else. We see light all the time—it's not inaccurate to say that it's all we see—illuminating the fetching features of Swedish actresses and directors, or alighting on a piece of paper taped to the cover of a book, and we have no idea what it is we are looking at.

I try to cherish this idea, of being wrong. It has not always been easy, because it is so pleasing and comfortable to be right, especially when it gives one the opportunity to say other people are wrong. But that light dawning, that small but potent vertigo as a beautiful idea, taken for granted, falls apart in one's mind, feels so very essential to the enterprise of literature, not only writing it but reading it and living in a world in which it is written and read. It's a ticket, being wrong, not only a citation but a way of gaining entrance to something more marvelous and exciting for my not knowing at all what it really is.

5

I like to think that
I killed him.

I'm eight years old, I think—young enough that I'm still playing with Fisher-Price people, tiny wooden dolls, armless and legless, spherical heads on a tubular bodies. My mother has a few standing up on the breakfast table, although one of them is about to topple down dead. That one is Carmen, of the opera *Carmen*. My mother is acting out the plot for me so that I'll be prepared for a free matinee performance in a nearby park, and sings a summary of José's last aria, right before he stabs our heroine, in an invented melody my family will sing for years:

> You *said*—
> you'd *be*—
> my *girlfriend!*

A lovers' triangle ending in murder, after detours into prostitution and smuggling, might not strike you as a piece of children's entertainment, but it was par for the course growing up.

My parents met at an opera performance, each of them on separate dates, and they held season tickets my whole life—indeed, my mother still has the same seats—leaving my sister and me to Saturday night television while they dressed up and went out, returning with stories of betrayal, conspiracy and tragedy by the bucketful. They enjoyed the lighter operas, too—bedroom farces with slamming doors and quick costume changes—but the best ones were the Italian classics, equal parts sordid melodrama and soaring music. Not content to sit in our seats and clap, most of my family ended up on the opera stage—my father finagled himself into a few nonspeaking, nonsinging roles, his role in *Tosca*'s church procession earning him a brief mention in a column in the *San Francisco Chronicle* as the world's first Jewish archbishop. My sister had a brief opportunity to appear as a silent Japanese ghost in *Turandot*, and I sang in the San Francisco Boys Chorus, the better to portray an assortment of urchins in various productions: urchins in the street in *La Bohème*, urchins at church in *Tosca*, urchins on a ship in *La Gioconda*, urchins playing solider in *The Queen of Spades*, urchins watching Carmen get murdered in *Carmen*. As puberty approached, my parents joked—I *think* they were joking—about extending my soprano career through castration, but in the long run I ended up with a passable baritone and a full set of secondary sex characteristics, both of which serve me fine.

I had piano lessons, too, from an endlessly patient man who taught me Bach and Mozart, but who preferred, as a performer, the music of Japanese avant-garde composers. We'd go to see him with various ensembles, attacking the piano to the accompaniment of shrieking fues, kotos of alternate tuning, and lots of gong action. I remember one performance in particular, for which my mother and I arrived early, chatting with each other as the musicians warmed up their instruments with picks and mallets, only to realize we had in fact arrived late and the performance had been in progress. I loved it, of course—nobody likes a gong more than a child—and it always puzzles me that most avant-garde music is kept away from young people despite their being an ideal audience. A friend of mine, a conductor of modern music, compared for me once the student matinee and evening performances of Morton Feldman's *Madame Press Died Last Week at Ninety*, which basically consists of a few musicians playing the same two notes over and over, very quietly. The young people thought this was great, and not only listened attentively but, the next day, sent in recordings of new pieces they'd written in Feldman's style, in memorial to various grandparents and pets. The adults fidgeted and wanted their money back.

All this lunatic music pleased me as a child, but like my parents I thought opera was best, not so much for the music, which was just all right—rarely enough gongs—but for the stories. I liked the madwoman throwing herself down the stairs, the seduction and double-crossing of the police inspector, the masked ball spoiled by impulsive homicide, the big love scene with the decapitated head of the holy man. It was a bit disappointing, as adolescence arrived and my first romances flopped around, to realize I'd never find a relationship with the reckless passion of

You *said*—
you'd *be*—
my *girlfriend!*

—a passion which was clearly the most compelling and exciting kind of relationship. Like everyone else, I had to learn the hard way that this was not so, that melodramatic tragedy was not actually a great way to, say, spend spring break. But it remained glorious onstage, on paper, onscreen and on the walls of my bedroom, where I had a small print of John Singleton Copley's painting *Watson and the Shark*. My parents let me take it home from a museum gift shop, after a small argument over whether or not it counted as a souvenir, given that the original painting was not in whatever museum we were visiting. But I didn't want the image to remember anything by. I just wanted to look at it, every morning while I tried to comb my hair.

The painting depicts a supposedly true event that happened to the man who commissioned it, when he was employed as a cabin boy in Havana and fell overboard, only to be attacked by a shark. It took some effort by the crew to rescue him successfully, and even then he lost a leg. None of this I knew then—indeed, I read this story just a few days ago. My childhood take on it was more complicated.

There are nine people aboard a small boat. In the water is a shark, and just inches away, naked and desperate, is a long-haired blonde person with one arm outstretched. For years I assumed this was a woman, and now the person reminds me of David Bowie on the cover of *Hunky Dory*. But what I found compelling about the painting were the people in the boat, who seemed to me bitterly divided. I saw two of them reaching down to help the woman who, like so many women in old paintings, was unnecessarily naked, with her legs discreetly crossed. But another passenger on the boat is pulling them back, to stop the rescue, and the person at the front of the boat, who seems in charge, is using a long oar to get farther away from the whole mess. Three other passengers to the left are shoving each other around, arguing over what course of action to take, and the only other person standing seems to be pleading with everyone to calm down, while the last passenger sits aloof, hardly noticing what is going on.

What was happening? I thought about it a lot. Why were some people reluctant to help this poor naked lady? The only explanation I could think of was that she was not a woman at all, but some kind of sea witch—a siren, a selkie, maybe some kind of saltwater nymph—who is trying to trick the gullible boaters into bringing her onboard, in the way that Dracula would slick back his hair and use his va-va accent to gain entrance to houses full of people full of blood. The captain, with his giant oar, knows better, I thought, as do some of the others. This explained why the woman was reaching for the shark—she was calling in reinforcements, comrades from the dark deep who share her predilection for shipwrecking. This made sense to a kid raised on opera, in which people sometimes worked out their differences via dagger and entombment.

When I look at it now I see much less. Everyone is trying to rescue poor Watson. Even the passenger, who seemed to me, for years, utterly uninterested, is in fact pale from fright. The oar is a harpoon, and the rescuers are only being clutched so that they don't fall in, too. It is a little puzzling why Watson is naked—is "cabin boy in Havana" a euphemism for an older profession?— and something about his frantic arm still looks wrong. But the extra layers of conspiracy and conflict that I dreamed up, gilding the lily of an already dramatic painting, are nowhere to be found in my heartless adult gaze. When I was a child it was all I saw.

I came by this honestly, from every angle. Being Jewish, for instance, meant learning the senseless stories of the Torah. Abraham and Isaac was my favorite, in which the patriarch takes his son to the top of the mountain to sacrifice him, only to be told at the last minute, by an angel no less, that it was a test. My father and I would take those walks to the library, and I would wonder if he would sacrifice me, if God—or G-d, as it was written in some of the Jewish books we had around the house, the word to me an unfinished game of hangman— asked him to? Would he tell me about it, as Abraham told Isaac, or would it be a surprise? Would anyone stop him and explain it was a test, or would I just get finished off, when we got to that clump of bushes, or the empty swing set in the park, still and spooky?

Maybe things were different now—Abraham and Isaac were a long time ago, I remembered—but there were recent stories too. My father, when he was my age—not the inscrutable cigar-smoker now, who might sacrifice me at any minute—was sent to play in the woods with his brother, whenever the Nazis knocked on the door. That's how he put it, *knocked on the door*, which helped me picture it—a tall house, silhouetted like the swing set, with Nazis knocking on the front door and my father and Uncle Mike, later in the balloon business, running out the back, into a vast shadowy mass of trees while the moon looked down at the scene, like an angel, wanting to say it was all a test. It was, in some ways, and we passed. My grandmother traded every-thing she could for a handful of diamonds, which she hid in the hollowed-out heel of her shoe, to parcel them out as bribes as needed on the journey out, and to start a life when they arrived in America. This was Jewish, too.

Over the years this story, like the woman in the painting not everyone wanted to rescue, has seemed a little embellished. That detail, the diamonds hidden in the heel of the shoe, feels maybe mythologized, the way it happens in families with the aviatrix great-grandmother, or the coin toss that grants you ship's passage, the distant ancestor who rescued the king's children from drowning. That last one, too, is from my family, but the other side—only once at a party I told it to someone, and they said someone in the English branch of *their* family saved the king's children from drowning. Lots of kings have children, and there are enough British ponds and fountains for them all to drown. Still, though, it seems unlikely it happened to both of our brave and quick-thinking ancestors.

But it wasn't only my ancestors in England, Germany, or Canaan. It was people around me, in the city where I lived. Even through my young eyes, San Francisco was a place rife with flourishing invention. Wherever I went, people seemed to be making things up. Culturally specific neighborhoods— Chinatown, the Italians in North Beach, the Mexicans in the Mission—put on spectacles that exaggerated or transformed traditions from their homelands—Chinese dragons for the New Year, bedecked in Pride flags, Días de los Muertos skeletons in the uniforms of local sports teams, a reenactment, canceled shamefully recently, of Columbus's discovery of America, something which never happened and certainly not in California. The Castro Theatre loomed large for me, just a few streetcar stops away from my house, a glorious art house theater which played *Nosferatu* with live, odd jazz accompaniment by the Club Foot Orchestra, or *Whatever Happened to Baby Jane?* with an audience of drag Joan Crawfords. And of course the entire Castro neighborhood was where people were inventing themselves, or maybe just finally had a space open enough to be who they were all along.

My soprano voice got me the title role in a few productions of the Christmas opera *Amahl and the Night Visitors*, for which I'd rehearse for weeks with cadres of local theatrical folk who had the expected mix, new to me then, of being queer, hilarious and damaged. I remember a deadpan actress who went by the name Houdini—no last name, thank you very much. I was too timid to talk to her much, but I overheard someone ask her if she was born with her name and she told them yes, but that she'd been born only recently, and that previously another person had lived in her body, but that she'd vanished from her old life—hence, Houdini. (Only years later did it occur to me that, of course, Houdini didn't vanish—he escaped.)

The basso in the show was a flouncy man, covered in scarves and quick with a joke—probably even quicker than I remember, as most of the jokes surely went over my head. After rehearsal he mentioned his wife was picking him up—even at thirteen this surprised me, because he seemed more like, um, the confirmed bachelor type. Who showed up was a magnificent looking person, heavily lipsticked and combat-booted, about whom I couldn't help asking, the next time I saw the singer, if, um, his wife was, er, a man.

"Of course not," he said.

"OK. Sorry."

He shrugged off my apology. "Daniel," he said, looking me right in the eyes. "We're who we are, not who we look like."

Who we are, not who we look like. It was a phrase that sat perfectly in my head, one foot in the shifting adolescent thoughts of identity and the other in the far-flung dramas of my favorite culture. It sounded conspiratorial, like a secret society, but brash and public, too. As the descendant of a woman who had hidden diamonds in her shoe and someone who had saved the king's children from drowning, and, further back genealogically, someone who agreed to sacrifice a child, it was no surprise that the stories that stayed in my head had the same flavor: larger than reality, more beautiful and fun, full of secrets and deceptions that, even when untrue, made the ordinary world I saw around me—*what the world looked like*—that much more interesting.

I saw this beauty at the opera, first in the audience after my mother had prepped me on the plots, and then from the wings, waiting to urchin myself around the stage. The character of Amahl in *Amahl and the Night Visitors* is an urchin further burdened with some undetermined leg problem, hobbling around the hovel—I still have the crutch from my first production—until the arrival of a Christmas miracle, both very predictable and extremely unrealistic. The people rehearsing around me, and the stories we were telling together, presented this kind of beauty—overblown, even garish, scent, light, rhythm, making the world much less loathsome.

This kind of beauty is so often reviled even though it seems to me everyone likes it as much as I do. "Unrealistic" is invariably an insult when applied to fiction, and yet the most popular stories, and the most lasting, are ripping yarns, full of impassable obstacles and boggling coincidences, even—maybe especially—the ones labeled "realistic." Famed realist authors resort to some of the farthest-fetched plots imaginable—Upton Sinclair and his convenient eaten-by-rodent plot device in *The Jungle*, Edith Wharton's *Ethan Frome* with its climactic suicide-by-sled twist—as part of their supposed dedication to chronicling gritty reality. One hears of the exhaustive research and consultation applied in Hollywood—you know, so the TV surgeons can use the precise medical terms in the episode where two separated twins accidentally reunite in the operating room. We keep watching, the way we pass along the sordid details in oft-repeated urban myths—the rat, mistaken for a small dog and adopted by the oblivious family, the scuba diver picked up by an airplane along with a large gulp of water to drop on a forest fire, leaving his charred, dead body in the ashen trees. These stories get repeated—we repeat them—not quite because we think they're true, but because the details glom on to us, like leeches. Gossip works the same way—we can't await to repeat whatever melodramatic item has dropped into our laps. The word is overused now, but these elements are *viral*, and they spread accordingly. They're not quite good stories, but they're the stuff of good stories, just a little bit better than truth—who we are, not what we look like. My parents didn't really meet at the opera, for instance—they recognized each other there, having met previously at a party and been unimpressed. But the opera story is better. Just saying that they met in the audience of a dramatic plot makes their meeting more dramatic.

During dinner breaks from opera rehearsals, I'd walk a few

blocks with the other boys in the chorus to a fast food restaurant, and if there was time I'd go across the street to a bookstore called A Clean Well-Lighted Place for Books, a Hemingway reference of which I was unaware. It was a good shop, extensive but curated, made all the more appealing to me because it was open late, until 11:00 p.m. I think—not that I was ever there that late; it just seemed magical that I could be. It was there I first encountered a writer and artist as influential to me as any other.

The books of Edward Gorey were filed in the humor section, which is how I found them at such a young age, although the booksellers probably just didn't know where to put them. Nobody did. Toward the end of his career, Gorey achieved a fair amount of iconic status, of the sort that befalls a few uncategorizable artists—that is, everyone pretending that they've loved them all along, and that the niche they're in has always been waiting for just that person. But most of the time he worked not quite in obscurity but in the face of public puzzlement, the questions around his work the ones all great works of art produce: *What is going on? Is the artist kidding? What is this, exactly?* When the first two volumes of *A Series of Unfortunate Events* were published, I sent copies to Gorey himself, after someone managed to get me the address of his house in Cape Cod, now a small, deadpan museum of his work. I enclosed a note saying how wild a fan I was of his books, and how I hoped he would forgive me for all I'd nicked from him. (I never heard back from Gorey, but shortly afterward he died. I like to think that I killed him.)

Gorey's little tomes look like picture books at first glance, and maybe they are. They generally consist of large pen-and-ink illustrations, with a few sentences of text as captions or on an otherwise blank page opposite. But rather than the usual stuff of picture books—simple stories, approachable language—we get sesquipedalian melodrama. The best example might be *The Blue Aspic*, which I purchased at the bookstore during the rehearsal break—the first book, I always say, that I purchased with my own money, by which I mean the allowance my father gave me.

The Blue Aspic has two threads—in one, a sequence of suspicious catastrophes assist a soprano, Ortezia Caviglia, in her rise to operatic fame, and in the other, her obsessive fan Jasper Ankle, already in destitute circumstances, falls into further squalor and desperation. The tone of the text switches from jokey ("The famous Spoffish emeralds were given to Caviglia by the Duke of Whaup") to mutely sad ("Jasper's gramophone got smashed as he was being evicted from his rooms"), and the illustrations, likewise, are full of the fanciful details of costumed glamor and the claustrophobic grays of poverty and institutionalization. The story is silly; the book is sad. If it's a joke, it's a sick one, but if it's serious, it's absurd. It is, of course, both-slash-neither, inhabiting an ambiguous and ambivalent space, in which Ortezia's frippery both lays bare Jasper's despairing circumstances and dares us to laugh at them. *The Blue Aspic* seems to propose that unrequited love is a form of inequity, although that idea, too, is both moving and moronic, and nothing that would have occurred to me as a child. I just kept staring at it.

It is no accident that much of my description of *The Blue Aspic*, then, could be applied to my own work—"a sequence of suspicious catastrophes" sounds like a bulky first draft of the title of my thirteen-volume orphan opus. I love *The Blue Aspic*, and I loved it when I was young; in return visits to A Clean Well-Lighted Place for Books and other bookshops, I began to collect these peculiar little Gorey books, whatever they were, and they occupied my mind a great deal. They seemed to be parodies, or maybe just homages, on something that seemed familiar and yet undefinable—old books and movies with suspicious millionaires, secret societies, murder and intrigue in mansions and garrets, not quite pinpointable in time or place past a certain old-fashioned European vibe—not true stories, but stories that ring true, the way the title is utter nonsense—aspic is nowhere to be found in *Aspic*—and yet perfectly mysterious and sinister. This is when I was reading Baudelaire, which had the same attractions—the overblown yet heartfelt rhetoric, the promise of an adventure both lurid and alluring—so to me these two artists are inextricably connected, but maybe I'm the only one making these connections. When I search online for Baudelaire references in Gorey's work, I only find articles about myself.

Early in my writing life, I found another artist who occupies this same slice of the Venn diagram, whose work became another signpost for me: Guy Maddin, a director whose movies have the look of old silent films, but somewhere in their old-timey camera moves, creaky visual effects and stagey acting, they convey heartfelt truths that hit me harder than so much glossy so-called realism. My favorite Maddin film, *Careful*, is about a small town in the mountains so susceptible to avalanche that all the citizens must speak in whispers and suppress all emotion, achieving a pressing tension in its exploration of domestic life; perhaps his most famous film, *The Saddest Music in the World*, concerns a contest to produce the most miserable piece of music, a loopy conceit that ends up being very moving, even as Isabella Rossellini loses her legs in an automobile accident and ends up with glass prosthetics filled with beer. How beautiful sadness can be and vice versa.

I saw Maddin speak once, introducing his favorite film, a 1927 silent called *The Unknown*. The film tells the story of Alonzo the Armless, a circus performer who secretly binds his arms to give his feet-centered knife tricks more realism. As luck would have it, the object of Alonzo's affection is a young woman who has a deep fear of arms, and the plot proceeds with various contrivances that make the initial premise seem a little tame. To call it a melodrama is to apply melodramatic understatement, but, as Maddin said from the podium—neither he nor I remember exactly what he said, which seems pretty perfect—only in melodrama can we see the world as it really is. The grandiose tropes of the overstated story are like the enlargement of photographs—which is what a projected film is, of course—the better to see the details that were there already. I watched *The Unknown* electrified, not just by the movie itself—which I've not only seen numerous times since but once provided its soundtrack at a screening, under the direction of the songwriter Stephin Merritt—but by this idea, vague in my mind for years, that Maddin had stated so clearly. It has guided me through all my work. My books have lots of murders, volcanos, pirates, ghosts, various monsters—and these are the ones for adults. Even my most "realistic" novels—*Why We Broke Up*, for instance, a teenage romance—have enormous, impossible elements in them, writ large, the best way to make clear a small truth—a love story, but sung loudly:

> You *said*—
> you'd *be*—
> my *girlfriend!*

When I started writing for children, I reread many of the books I had loved, and like absolutely every writer, stole the things I liked. *The Bad Beginning*, book the first in *A Series of Unfortunate Events*, begins with the three young heroes, not yet orphans, riding a trolley to the beach, where they learn of their parents' death in a fire. I put something melodramatic at the end of the trolley ride not just to get the story going, but as quiet homage to my own histrionic imagination, which was applied to a book I'd found on my shelf at home. The book is *The Moffats*, by Eleanor Estes, one of several novels about a set of siblings who live in modest circumstances with their mother in a small Connecticut town during the First World War. The Moffat books belong to a genre of children's literature which offers readers a look at a vanished time in history, and *The Moffats* presents such antiquated exhibits as rationed food, scarlet fever and a trolley ride, which has, thanks to some carelessness at the switch, two trolley cars riding toward each other on the same track. Estes strikes a perfect tone, easy to admire and difficult to emulate, that moves easily from interior monolog to roving observation, the way it is when you tell someone a story:

The children looked at one another. Excitement! They looked ahead. Way, way down the car line, under the arch of elm trees, they could see it now! Could see the other trolley coming right towards them! Just a little speck it was at the other end of Second Avenue. But bigger and bigger as it drew near. The nearer it came, the more excitedly the motorman clumped down on his bell. Pretty soon they were near enough to hear the other motorman clump down on *his* bell.

Although their hearts began to beat fast, Joe, Jane, and Rufus said and did nothing. The others in the trolley, roused out of their lethargy, first ran to the motorman and implored him to stop. But the motorman was deaf to all entreaties. So the passengers all ran to the back of the car to get as far as possible from what looked like an inevitable crash. Some uttered silent prayers.

And imagine what this looked like to people along Second Avenue! Windows were thrown up and amazed heads stuck out of them. Everybody on the street stopped to stare and wave their arms about in excitement. Old Mrs. Squire, who was carrying a basket of apples to her nephew, grew so frantic she actually threw apples at the motorman and screamed, "Go back, go back."

We move from the young heroes in the trolley down to the approaching threat, back to the inside of the car, up to the windows and down to old Mrs. Squire, who pops up several times in the book as panicky comic relief, the pace maintained by those jumpy sentence fragments—"Excitement!" "But bigger and bigger as it drew near"—which bump up against the tricky vocabulary, to a young reader anyway, of "lethargy," "entreaties" and "inevitable." Sentences that, in a different context, could be labeled experimental—"Windows were thrown up and amazed heads stuck out of them"—fit right in, and most of all, the three heroes say and do nothing. How can they? They're children. As a child, so attuned was I to Estes's breathless description that my mind, fed by opera and aspic, expected something truly terrible to happen. As an adult reader, I know of course that this incident, one of many in an episodic book that begins a series about a family, will not end in tragedy, as it should not and does not. But in that loose-limbed space in the childhood mind of a reader, it seemed like there might be an horrific accident. It seemed, to me, like a better story, and so in adulthood I put three children back on a trolley and began the Baudelaire children's parade of misfortune. *A Series of Unfortunate Events* drags three orphans through life's turbulent landscape—something they first observe silently, in shock and suspense, seeing and doing almost nothing, and then, as unfortunate events continue, become more and more active, much to their own detriment. The Baudelaires face deceit and blackmail, murder and kidnapping, and then, beginning to solve the codes and riddles of childhood, find that their own deceit and blackmail frame them for murder themselves. They end up cast out of the world, shipwrecked and desperate as poor Watson in the print that hung on my wall. The adults around them are corrupt, and as the children become adults as well, they're corrupted, too. We all are. The more we participate in the world, the more culpable we become for the mess and troubles we face. When we are young, we are shocked at the world's insistence that it can only be thus, full of suffering and injustice; as we age, our shock is when we can change anything at all before the curtain rings down. The only way to present this idea was to show it enormously, showily, with exaggeration and theatrics, the better to see who we are, and not, maybe *never*, what we look like.

6

Why did I keep cutting this?

Here's an incident in my life that has almost appeared in every other chapter of this book. I keep cutting it. I was young—eight, I'm guessing, maybe ten—and, during some school break I think, was signed up for a little class taught in the basement of one of the city's big museums. I was dropped off early, maybe—anyway, I was alone, and many surrounding details have escaped me. But I remember the man and what he did.

First he just talked to me, and he was instantly creepy enough that I didn't want him to. I moved away, toward the educational exhibits that were in this little basement room, while he kept asking whatever it was he was asking. I can remember the exhibits pretty well, and am not describing them so you won't know which museum it was, the better not to associate it with a ghastly assault in their basement years and years ago. They're not to blame, of course. I just slipped somehow through a net, privileged and thoughtful, that otherwise did a pretty good job of keeping me from harm.

He kept at me, kept talking, stepping closer and then pressing closer. I remember steadfastly refusing to believe my realization of what it was my hand was gripping, being made to grip by the hand gripping mine. I have a tactile memory of something off with my clothes, not quite undressed but partway, something tucked wrong maybe, or the sensation of air on some part of my body that should have been covered. I wasn't fucked, just messed with, best he could against whatever frozen, silent resistance I managed to put up. And then it was done, gruntingly, warm and sticky with me not knowing what it was—my biggest clue to just how young I was when this happened—that was on me.

More people came into the room, and on top of whatever bad struggling thing that had just happened to me was layered a newer, more familiar struggle, that of hurriedly pretending everything was OK. Children learn this early. I remember the man saying something I knew wasn't true—some excuse, some alibi—and then whomever else was around took me to where the class was starting. I couldn't have been as much of a mess as I thought, or perhaps the other person just couldn't, wouldn't, see it. In the class they were showing a movie, and I remember I kept looking behind me, still damp from it, back past the beam of the projector to the man framed in the doorway. I suppose he was making sure I wasn't going to tell, but I didn't know that then. I just knew that then, especially right then, I was very scared. That was the scary part.

Why did I keep cutting this? I wasn't sure where it belonged. I couldn't really connect it to anything. For many years, I kept forgetting it happened, losing track of it the way you might someone's name or a place you visited once, and while it now seems firmly ensconced in memory, I can't really measure its effect. It feels ridiculous to say *not much*, an answer I'd have trouble believing from someone else. But among the things that steal sleep from me, that upset me despite the passage of time and impossibility of changing the past, this ranks very low, and while my psyche is hardly free of peculiarities, I don't know which ones seem reasonably born out of being attacked in a basement. It feels dishonest to omit it, but the incident kept not finding its place in the other chapters. It just floats around the book the way it floats in my life—present but unattached, like a balloon.

There is, in fact, a specific balloon I'm thinking of. When I was in high school I sat with my friends on a bench outside a diner, waiting for a table to open up. It was pretty late, which is why we were there: the diner didn't really have anything to say for itself besides being open twenty-four hours a day and being named after a movie we liked, *Baghdad Cafe*. We were huddled a bit while we talked—it was cold out—and then a balloon bounced by. It was nothing fancy, not a helium one, just a regular balloon that you might blow up quick for a party. One of us caught it and we saw there was something written on the side in felt pen: *Hello*. We looked around: on another bench, also waiting, was a sour-faced couple paying no attention to us, but otherwise the street was quiet. Then another showed up, with another message, and another with another, and again. We were laughing, looking up at nearby windows or roofs, down the windy block looking for the source, and then a green one arrived, the one I think about most, with the message *To Match Her Sweater*. One of my friends had a green sweater on, and now we knew the balloons were really for us, not some colorful accident. Then our table was ready and we went inside, but over ice cream and fries one friend confessed: the balloonists were the stone-faced couple on the bench, who relied on our friend to distract us at key moments in their improvised, gossamer prank.

Many things are like this, I think—mysterious moments large and small, happy and terrifying, their source inexplicable even when revealed. Thinking about the man who assaulted me is a handful of questions—about how he found such opportunities and exploited them, how he wrested away whatever qualms he might have had, and above all his motivation, terrible and presumably born out of something equally awful. There aren't any satisfactory answers, just like there's no real reason some couple, who maybe found forgotten balloons in their bag—I'm making this up—decided to mystify a group of laughing kids. I think about the assault about as often as I think of that balloon, *To Match Her Sweater*, just floating, connected to nothing. I can't put it in place.

This is a familiar feeling, as a writer. Each book of mine is something I couldn't stop thinking about, or really a collection of them, stuck together like burrs that are also stuck to me. I try to find a place for them on paper, and then of course there is the other world of books, more tiresome to think about and live through, in which one tries to find a place for the book in the world. All this can take a long time. When I open my books, certain ideas and phrases look like exhausted, triumphant travelers, having come a long, long way to rest on the page. In my novel *Why We Broke Up*, for instance, a boy and girl in high school have this post-virginity conversation:

"Was that time better?" you said.

"It's supposed to hurt," I said.

"I know," you said, and put both hands on me. "But, I guess I mean, but what is it like?"

"Like putting a whole grapefruit into your mouth."

"You mean it's tight?"

"No," I said, "I mean it doesn't fit. Have you ever tried to put a whole grapefruit into your mouth?"

The laughing was the best part.

This conversation, basically word for word, was something a friend related to me in high school, about a talk she had with her boyfriend. Her boyfriend was quite a few years older, and although my friend and I were very close, I never met him. Their relationship was in a different space than where she and I spent time, giggling in gym class and wandering used bookstores. He had picked her up at a café, by noticing what she was reading and asking if she thought Milan Kundera was a misogynist, which was obviously the sexiest and most glamorous thing that had ever happened to anyone. When she told me about the grapefruit talk it was startlingly intimate, which is one reason why it stuck in my head, and ended up in a draft of my first novel. *The Basic Eight* is about a murder in a high school and the resultant media circus it inspires, which was inspired in turn by a murder I read about when I was in high school, and its increasingly irresponsible coverage. It being the '80s, it was only a matter of time before Satanism was part of the speculations—this was, after all, when human sacrifice was being regularly and falsely reported and prosecuted in day care centers—only to have the revealed motivation to be much less exciting: somebody didn't like somebody else. That answer, expected but somehow disappointing, was what stuck with me, and as I started the novel I gathered other high school details that were floating around my mind. I remembered my friend's postcoital talk with her boyfriend, a relationship which, now that I was no longer in high school, seemed less glamorous and more fraught. Gradually, *The Basic Eight* became about the secrets we keep when we're young, about how easy and uneasy is to remain silent about what seems both obvious and inexpressible, written at an age when I was beginning to learn more about the people I'd spent late nights with, laughing, outside diners. In the end, "It doesn't fit" didn't seem to fit. Out it went, to bounce around my brain for another decade or so.

I spent some of those years trying to find a place for *The Basic Eight*—that is, my literary agent tried to sell it while I waited and worried. The same well-furnished net that kept me mostly from harm put me within shouting distance of other people who had literary agents, which was lucky, and it was lucky which one I got recommended. Her name, Charlotte Sheedy, can be found on the dedication page of *Why We Broke Up*, and on the dedication pages and lists of acknowledgments of countless other books. She is a tremendously skilled agent, but her real knack is helping people find their places in the world. After someone recommended her, I sent Charlotte some pages from *The Basic Eight* when I was midway through writing it, prompted not so much by a sense that it was time to try and sell it as much as by a sense that it would be really really great if it sold. A few weeks later she happened to be in San Francisco and invited me to a drink at her hotel. I did not know what this meant, but I dressed up for it. We sat down and she asked if I liked Old-Fashioneds and I said yes, of course, not having the faintest idea what that meant either. A sandwich? A type of novel? A professional arrangement? Not until mine arrived on a tray did I learn it was a cocktail, which made me think everything was going to be all right. Gently, she suggested that I finish writing the novel before trying to sell it, advice I wrote down in a little notebook I'd bought for the meeting, and I remember returning to my apartment that evening, dizzy with bourbon and sugar, to get right to it.

Some months later a draft was done, grapefruit scene and all, and I visited her office in New York when I was in town for a Bat Mitzvah. Manhattan was discombobulating to me—I couldn't afford taxis and couldn't understand the subway, so I walked a great distance and arrived early to sit at the coffee place around the corner for an hour or so, making myself more jittery and more broke. Upstairs in her office she said she thought there was a place for this novel—she put it just like that—and I remember coming back out to the streets of New York and dancing happily on one of those gratings you're not supposed to step on. I moved to New York shortly afterward, with a plan hardly more specific than enjoying the launch of my literary career. My girlfriend, now my wife, had a slightly more sensible plan of attending graduate school, but that meant I was alone all day with nothing to do. Back in San Francisco, I'd lived very cheaply and had saved quite a bundle of money, off of which I planned to live for maybe a year as my literary fortunes rose. This money of course managed to vanish in minutes, and I scrambled around with various freelance gigs, which kept my head above water, in the way that a drowning person's head is also, during their fruitless struggle, above water. I started walking to Charlotte's office to see how my career was going—several times a week. I cannot believe this was something I did, dropping by the offices of a high-profile literary agent unannounced every few days, when I had no actual business with her whatsoever. Out of pity, or maybe just to get me out of there, she began paying me to read other manuscripts that came her way for possible representation, which seems akin to asking a nun where one might find a really good strip club. I would sit at home reading hopeful novels and memoirs, wondering if I could possibly spot success from where I was sitting. I doubted it. It was becoming a routine now, to stop by her office to drop off manuscripts and pick up a small check and a new rejection letter. Editors were writing to me—or sometimes to David Handler, a sure sign they were reading carefully—care of Charlotte, to say there was not in fact a place for my book. More than once, I, a grown man, cried on the sofa in Charlotte's office, which she later offered to me as a gift. It was better than any I could afford.

Out of further pity, she helped me organize a reading series for writers who couldn't get published. We called it Refusé, after the Salon de Refusé, the French art show in 1863 which featured artists rejected by the establishment. I chose the other writers from the manuscripts I was reading, Charlotte invited young editors who were afraid to say no to her, and every month, on an off-night in a Soho theater space to which Charlotte donated heavily, I introduced a handful of writers by reading out loud from their rejection letters. We had a lot of fun and nobody sold anything. The alumni list from Refusé is pretty impressive, but none of them are writers who found their place in that way, including me. We were like the scraps of paper on which I'd written things like "grapefruit doesn't fit," and then wondered where in the world they should go.

I saved that scrap for years, until I found myself writing another book about high school. By this time, my research into high school students came less from memory and more from eavesdropping on public transportation, although the word "eavesdropping" is a little too active for just being invisible to chatting high school friends—not too surprising, given that when I was their age, an adult would have had to blow up a balloon to get my attention. The rhythm of their talking, the revelations and jokes and the slang and the stutters, was excellent material, and I often departed the bus muttering some phrase over and over until I reached a surface flat enough to open my notebook and write it down. Paging through *Why We Broke Up*, I can see these little fragments everywhere, repurposed, polished up, recostumed like character actors you saw two weeks ago in King Arthur's court, but who now work at the tech company in a romantic comedy. When I spot the grapefruit dialog, I look past those lines to the first place I tried to write them, in a novel that took years to sell (during which the lines were cut), past that to when I first heard them, one of countless conversations and memories from that lifelong friendship, one of many, many things stuck in my head.

By the time *Why We Broke Up* was published, I was in a different place. Charlotte had helped me find it. In her desperation to sell *The Basic Eight*, she had passed the novel to some children's editors, and now two years after I was reading rejection letters out loud in a downtown theater space to no discernible effect, I was at a chain bookstore in Lansing, Michigan. The place was the size of an airplane hangar, in which rows and rows of folding chairs had been set up and two seats occupied, in the back, by adults. It was the first event on the first tour for the first Lemony Snicket books. I had prepared a whole shtick, which included performing a song, "Scream and Run Away," that Stephin Merritt had written for me in exchange for one hundred dollars cash I'd fetched from the ATM. I couldn't really afford to part with one hundred dollars, but he needed the money as much as I did. Now in Lansing I was performing it for two adults, who came up to me afterward to say they were buyers from the rival chain bookstore across town, and that they found my work so gallingly inappropriate, they had to see what sort of monster was responsible. This seemed about right to me. Charlotte had finally sold *The Basic Eight* for the least amount of money she had ever negotiated for a book of fiction, and now two volumes about sad orphans in horrific trouble in a world fashioned by my own literary obsessions were failing, to no one's surprise if only because there was no one there to witness it, in Lansing. Even published, my books, I thought, were like a grapefruit in someone's mouth. They didn't fit.

But the world of publishing, it is too often forgotten, is not the world of literature, which is sustained not in buildings stuffed with hopeless folding chairs but in the imagination. This is especially true in childhood. You never love a book the way you love a book when you are ten. Anyone can open a book, but it is easier for a child to step into it, to float in the world of the story, which in turn opens up to include the reader in ways we largely forget as adults. As a child, you can walk around imagining yourself the hero of the book you're reading, or perhaps a whole overlapping world, a new plot thread, a way to participate in the story you love. The book has a place for you.

From Lansing I went to a few more cities, and began to see signs that this sort of literary success, the most important and least visible kind, was maybe sprouting here and there. Hardly anyone showed up, but they were all interested in just the right way. I always said that Lemony Snicket couldn't be there at the bookstore, that I was his official representative and thus a guaranteed disappointment, and the young people grasped at once that I was somebody pretending to be somebody pretending to be somebody. This created a space in which we could talk about the troubles of the Baudelaire orphans not quite as if they were real but as if they were really happening. These first readers were worried about them. Far from home, flush with failure and queasy from eating at airports, I had the same worry. One girl had dressed as Violet Baudelaire by recreating her signature move: using a ribbon to tie up her hair, which was not long enough to be tied up in a ribbon. One boy leaned close to me and told me, chapter by chapter, the entire plot of *The Reptile Room*; another, when I asked if he wanted me to personalize the autograph by adding his name, told me that he wouldn't want to be associated with such dreadful stories. "Just like someone else of my acquaintance," he said meaningfully, and walked out of the store without looking back. There was a place for these books, I saw, even if it wasn't on a best-seller list. In fact, the *New York Times* had just started a children's best-seller list, and one of my editors solemnly explained to me why I wouldn't be on it. A few weeks later four of the top ten books were mine, bewildering everyone. I went to the movies and heard two people, strangers in the row in front of me, discussing the Baudelaires. Bookstores began to have contingency plans, for when a child, excited to meet me, threw up, and we shared the best contingency plans—sawdust, scented candles—with other bookstores. My wife and I bought a house, and then flew off to a literary festival, where I presented my work to a screaming crowd on the largest stage. People—thousands of *strangers*—were interested in whatever it was I was doing. The corporate sponsor ran out of copies of my books to sell, a situation unheard of at a literary event and so contrary to the company's ethos that I thought the rep was going to cry when she told me the news. The artist who preceded me was a dinosaur, by which I don't mean an author older than I was, with an out-of-date style. I mean Barney, from children's television. "Faulkner had the same slot," I kept telling friends in the authors tent.

What had happened, what was still happening, was a dream come true for any author, and indeed this felt like an actual dream, some surreal mash-up of autobiography and genre tropes you only half remember in the morning, actually springing to life—a blessing to be sure, a spectacular gift, albeit one like golden shoes, that you never thought you'd get because nobody gets golden shoes. I would utter the phrase "Lemony Snicket" in conversation, but now instead of a blank look in reply, I was increasingly getting frowns of confusion or even derision. The phrase had found a place in the culture unattached to a real person—it was like saying I was another author at the festival, Spider-Man, who, no joke, followed me onstage. When *The*

Basic Eight was published, no literary festival wanted me—most humiliatingly, I was booked on a panel called First Time Success Stories only to be told there wasn't a place for me after all. Now I went all the time, and I liked them. I liked the variety of authors there, the places literature had found for them and their work, journalists and chefs, extraordinary events chronicled by memoirists or dreamt up by fiction writers, unknown poets proclaimed by other unknown poets to be overpublicized, all bumping elbows and shaking hands. Over the years, I watched these writers shift places as they tried new genres or won prizes, and I traced my own path, from something of a young upstart to something like an old man. I liked when we all had to catch a ride together—a shuttle to wherever the festival had gathered their white tents, or a convoy of cars, driven by bookish volunteers, to take us to some dinner or reception. We'd gather in the lobby, at first standing apart but then, recognized via nametag, meeting people we'd never otherwise encounter, reuniting with writers we knew, introducing a friend to another friend to the friend of a stranger, the circle getting larger and louder with the awkward goodwill of people mostly used to working alone, hugs and handshakes colliding as more and more arrived. "It's turning into an orgy," was my go-to joke for such friendly, unwieldy times, until I was publicly chastised by another children's author for saying such a horrid thing. (By strange coincidence, I had written a critical review of her work some years previous.) "It probably didn't occur to you," she said, "that some of the women in the lobby were likely survivors of sexual assault."

I'm sure she thought she was putting me in my place. It did not occur to her that the specter of sexual assault she raised would be my own. Reading her denunciation of me onscreen, I felt the sudden shift, as I did in the museum basement, of a friendly and deeply harmless scene into a threatening situation. The realization that what you thought was a safe place was in fact something dangerous was as frightening in adulthood as it was in childhood. It became simple to compare them, because I watched it happen, as an adult, to my own child.

We were vacationing in Italy and my son, fidgety after a big meal in a famous restaurant, wanted to walk back alone maybe half a mile through the city to the hotel while my wife and I lollygagged around the fountains and alleys. When we returned to the hotel he wasn't there. We went back out into the summer night, crowded with tourists and nightlife, our situation both fraught and ridiculous. The area was a privileged playground, safe, welcoming and luxurious. The streets were crammed with other families, lots of English speakers, and our son was smart and good, sure to ask politely for help and not to stumble into trouble. He wasn't even that young, and he was wearing a conspicuous hat, a proud new traveler's purchase. Still, though, where the fuck was he? I knew he would be OK—the alternative, as I circled around and doubled back to those few square blocks, was too monstrous to entertain—but the lights, the laughter, even a sparkly carnival ride like a too-perfect detail in a thriller, grew garish and finally nightmarish in the hour or so before he found his way back. It had been my job to keep him safe, to build a net like the one that had sustained me for my childhood; like me, he'd discovered his net had a hole or two.

Recalling it now I think of a bit of literature—of course I do—that comes to mind whenever I am feeling lost. It is a passage from Benjamin Anastas's quiet masterpiece *The Faithful Narrative of a Pastor's Disappearance*, which, it seems worth mentioning, preceded a lost decade of doubt and sadness for the author:

By the time she made it back to the same corner from her hotel room the rain had stopped, and the million-plus lights of the new Times Square filled the air with a saccharine glow, making everything, even her own reflection in the plate-glass doors of the Virgin Megastore, seem vague and artificial. She averted her eyes from that shadow of herself as she passed by, ignoring the uniformed security guard who murmured *Yeah, baby* and stepped aside to get a better look at her figure. *Where do people come from? And where do they go? Who makes a world this unbearable?* she thought, walking through the center of an unfamiliar city, and she wondered, once again, how Thomas could have left her alone to survive, well, *this* . . . Bethany walked the confines of Times Square in a kind of circle, searching every face she passed for evidence of human kindness, and encountering more varieties of skin tone, age, expression, style, and character than she could quantify—and looking for Thomas in every one. *All those people,* she thought, standing outside the soulless Marquis on Broadway and trying, without much luck, to block out the ranting minister from the 12 Tribes of the Nation of Israel, *all those people,* she thought, looking up at the painted sign for the Heavenly Coffee, and down at the smiling image of Tiger Woods, *all those people,* she thought, turning back to the crowded sidewalk, *and not one of them is him.*

The clutter and clamor, the way Anastas absolutely stuffs the page with details both specific and abstract, congruous and irrelevant, with that fierce focus beating beneath it as the heroine looks for the titular man, a runaway or abductee, someone lost or vanished amidst *all those people, all those people, all those people.*

In the years since, I've watched my son tell the story of that night, casting it, as one does, in all sorts of lights, at all sorts of angles. I've heard it as a story of triumph and ingenuity, in which a young man who didn't speak Italian nevertheless managed to communicate his situation to a stranger, a story of parental panic, co-starring two deadpan cops in hilarious uniforms, a story illustrating why one needs the latest phone at all times regardless of cost, a story of fear, of adventure, of what might have happened and still might happen next time. He's still finding a place for it. I'd like to think this is the most discombobulating thing in his life, the most troublesome moment to process. But of course I know better. I knew better even before I ended up in a museum basement, struggling and confused, that our stories are not just full of incident and detail with which we struggle to make sense, but in fact the struggle is the story. The places for us are the places we find, and meanwhile we send our stories out into the world in one way or another, so they might float someplace, not as lessons or even messages, but just another colorful scrap that might align with something that, to someone maybe, already makes a sort of sense. *To Match Her Sweater.* Catch it and then, as we did that night, let it go its own way down the street, to a place out of sight.

7

The blanks we find
in the world.

When my son was approaching teenaged life, I was vaguely aware the skilled parents are supposed to start conversations about difficult topics earlier rather than later, so I instituted regular talks on various sexual and/or chemical issues. Our conversations had four rules:

1. My son would choose from a narrow list of topics (sex, drugs, drinking, romance, body, assorted culture).
2. I would speak briefly on the topic of his choice.
3. He would ask at least one question.
4. We would both be mortified the entire time.

—and for the first of these conversations, his chosen topic was alcohol. After a couple of minutes in which I droned on about its addictive qualities, the wallops it gives your health, how it leads to bad choices, especially for tender youths, it was time for him to ask a question, and his was very sensible. "If it's so bad for you, why do we have it?"

Parenting is a pop quiz on the world. Again and again you are asked about things of which you know zero, often things you haven't really thought about, and they are often things you *should* have thought about, basic crucial omnipresent things. And these inquiries are coming, often without warning, from someone who assumes, despite increasing and eventually overwhelming evidence to the contrary, that not only do you know the answers but have them all handy, that you are more than qualified, you are expert, somehow, at telling them what's what. And of course you don't know anything.

This would be a tricky needle to thread, I knew. My son had learned the word *drunk* at our Passover table. Per tradition, everyone would consume four glasses of wine, and our family had augmented the Haggadah with a reading from Baudelaire.

> One should always be drunk. That's all that matters; that's our one imperative need. So as not to feel Time's horrible burden that breaks down your shoulders and bows you down, you must get drunk without ceasing.
>
> But what with? With wine, with poetry, or with virtue, as you choose. But get drunk.

If it's so bad for you, why do we have it? Well, I began making up a story, filling in the blanks from who knows what, about two tribes of people who lived on opposite sides of a mountain, close but wary neighbors, and when they got together—here my spitballing was getting much worse—at the top of the mountain, to talk about, oh, I don't know, sharing the watering hole—*watering hole?*—well, it went better if they had a few sips of something fermented, in a bronze pot or a clay jug. Everyone would relax then.

My son gave me a look, wondering what we all wonder about our parents—*who are you?* What I wanted to tell him was much truer than some story I'd probably tossed together from middle-school skimming the works of Jean M. Auel looking for the sex scenes. Truth be told, my son had already experienced the thrill of alcohol. He just didn't remember. When he was younger, he was one of the few child guests at a wedding we attended. He was not having a particularly good time. The couple had wanted him there, but after the initial flurry of cooing attention he was soon cast away, wandering around the rented mansion answering the same old questions—name, age, location of school—and then drifting back to us, whereupon we'd shoo him toward whomever hadn't asked him those things yet. The cake was served, and he asked us how many pieces he could have. With the laissez-faire parenting brought on by laughing with friends whilst sipping champagne, we said: as much as you want. Then the music started, and our son, normally low-key at such events, began to dance. He danced so wildly, showily, confidently that a small crowd gathered to cheer him on. My wife and I wondered what we all wonder about our children: *Who are you?* Then, with a bite of cake, I solved the mystery. The happy couple had asked a friend to make a rum cake—not the kind that tastes a little rummy around the edges, but the kind that is soaked, post-baking, in rum. My son was soused, a soused fourth grader at a wedding. Though he had no memory of it—he would soon be asleep for ten hours—my teenage son had already had the classic experience of drinking too much at a wedding and making a spectacle of himself on the dance floor, as tribes on a mountaintop have done for generations.

For Californians of a certain stripe, the experience of alcohol and weddings is more specific. I am talking about wineries. The wineries, some of them anyway, are very beautiful, with sloping hills of vines growing on those skeleton sticks, and views of other wineries, also beautiful. In the fall and spring, the weather is perfect, so couples reserve the weekends and send out invitations. And then it's summer, time for the actual wedding, and the sun pelts down on the hill and there is not a speck of shade to be found. You, the Californian wedding guest, have arrived on time and all dressed up, must do a quick calculation of how much white wine, being passed on little round trays, will bring on the welcome glow enabling you to think of true love and a lifetime of happiness instead of your own sweaty feet and armpits, without drinking so much that you will become dehydrated and cranky and unable to find joy in the string quartet's half-audible Vivaldi. If there is any kind of delay—if, say, the priest arrives on time but the rabbi is late, making it look bad for your team—the trays make the rounds again, and the stakes get higher.

Once, faced with such escalating circumstances, I took shelter in the air-conditioned tent, as the ceremony went on. The couple were of the same sex, in the early days of marriage equality, which meant that in addition to the usual rigamarole, there were some additional readers testifying to the historic significance of the lengthy occasion in the searing heat. I sat discreetly at a table where some prepared materials were waiting for later. The couple was going on an extensive, extravagant honeymoon, with many glamorous stops, and guests were encouraged to write some well-wishing on some pre-stamped postcards, addressed to various chic hotels. I obliged, and then it occurred to me that I know many of the guests' names, and that the couple, in this digital age, was unlikely to recognize anyone's handwriting. A postcard could be a perfect vehicle not only for well-wishing but for confessions, increasingly hysterical in tone, of secret longings, shocking escapades, perhaps even murder. The couple might find it interesting to read, after a long romantic day in Paris or Istanbul, some inflammatory gossip, descriptions of long-hidden spiritual rituals, or even angry threats, from the people they knew and loved most. By the time the tent was in full party mode, I'd ghostwritten twenty or thirty messages with enough revelations for ten seasons of television, in addition to my own signed, undramatic "mazel tov."

It was a writing exercise of sorts, fueled by a reckless incaution that's sometimes difficult to drum up when I'm writing a book. I've been working so long in literature that it can on occasion feel like work. My sentences lump up and don't do anything interesting. And then I think of those postcards and am reminded that the best prompting a writer needs is blank paper, waiting for someone to fill it in. I taught a weeklong poetry writing workshop, ages ago, in which Monday's exercise was to write a poem with the word *bathtub* in it. (I like the word *bathtub*.) Over the week, more and more words were required, until the list was actually cribbed from a John Ashbery poem, the words of which I put into alphabetical order. On Friday, I gave everyone a pocket dictionary—a reminder of the countless tools, the everlasting blank space, with which and on which we get to play. I can't drink and write—I've tried—but I can try to court the brash recklessness, the blurring of boundaries, which comes from tipsiness.

A case can be made that composing new poems and hogging a bunch of postcards to forge scandalous messages from other people are two entirely different enterprises, but my comeuppance was delivered before the wedding was through. Shortly before last call, a few of the other guests, flushed from disco, stripped to their underwear and took a presumably refreshing dip in an ornamental pool. Security asked for their names, as they would be banned from this particular winery for life. One guest, Andrew Sean Greer, indulged in a creative exercise of his own, and gave the name "Daniel Handler."

By then, my wife and I were long back in our overdecorated room in the bed and breakfast. At such weddings, the issue of where to stay can be tricky. Sad is the guest who agrees not to drink, the better to drive various tipsy friends back home late at night. The inns are scattered hither and yon, and you never quite know what you're in for. We'd found a small bed and breakfast a short taxi's distance away, run by a married couple who straightaway asked us, after we'd volunteered that we were attending a wedding, if we were married, too. This struck me as a bad question to ask when you're in the rented-bed-in-an-obscure-location business, but we pled guilty. This made them very happy. Wasn't it a blessing? (To be married? Sure.) It was a miracle, didn't we agree? (Um, sure, absolutely.) It was a miracle, they insisted, of course it was, to have found each other. (We're tired, is that the key there in your hand?) People often said things like this, to my wife and me, especially early in our marriage, asking us to agree on it being a miracle. It always sounds a little insulting, as if both of us are so incredibly freakish that the chances of our pairing up are spectacularly slim—two odd-ball creatures, nearly the last of some species, who miraculously found mates.

Upstairs in the doily-smothered bedroom was a basket of magazines dedicated to marriage, which we read to each other while the wine wore off. They displayed that smooth, plastic tone in which American evangelical culture pretends to be normal, in order to lure secular souls. The innkeepers' insistence on miraculousness seemed clearer now. My wife dozed off and seemed unglad when I woke her to read a suggested tip for keeping a marriage fresh: that one morning you leave the house early, to arrive at your husband's workplace—of course, only husbands have workplaces—ahead of him, and decorate his desk by writing his name in rose petals. To this date, she has done no such thing, although admittedly with my desk being mere steps from the breakfast table, it'd be tricky to pull off. In any case, we are happy without it. I turned off the light and drifted to sleep under twenty-odd coverlets pondering the sort of marriage such a thing would enliven.

But of course every marriage is its own mystery. When my wife and I were even younger, we lived in Manhattan in an astonishingly large sublet apartment—that is, a regular-sized apartment which is thus astonishingly large for New York City. As a result, we were asked to host a wedding party, for a friend whose friends we didn't know very well. She was marrying a surprising person, out of the blue, and the first half of the party consisted of everyone trying to find out which of us knew anything about this new husband. Nobody did, so the second half of the party was gin-soaked, the better to garner the appropriate amount of joy, instead of confusion, about what had just happened. In particular I spent blurry time with the officiant—a vicar, something I'd sort of thought you couldn't be unless you were in a British novel. He in fact was British, although his church was sending him to Italy soon, where he would be ensconced in an enormous villa he insisted my wife and I visit. We never saw him again, though. Later in the festivities, he slipped out with another guest to have sex in the stairwell of our apartment building. They returned to the party, and the other guest found his roommate to brag about his clerical conquest. The roommate was standing with the vicar's wife, and although this passed largely unnoticed at the party, the ensuing drama carried all these people out of our orbit. I pasted this incident, more or less, into my novel *Bottle Grove*, which explores the mysterious muddle of marriage. Opening with this wedding scene, with one marriage betrayed while another one begins, seemed to me perfectly emblematic of marriage's utter and unpredictable unknowability, not only in the novel but in real life, where the couple celebrating the wedding are no longer together, but the vicar and his wife are, at least last I checked.

A story I tell about my wife and me is that early in our relationship, we spent a few days in Vermont at an inn where they thankfully didn't inquire about our marital status. We did the usual things, driving around looking at cows and foliage by day, rolling around in the bathtub (see?) and four poster

bed by night. One afternoon we found a used bookstore—
one of those big cavernous ones with towers of tomes everywhere and one cranky man who doesn't want to help you. The
prescribed thing to do, of course, would have been to walk
hand in hand through the place, a new couple cutely oohing
together over favorite titles. But we were not fucking around.
We were both mad for literature and needed to comb savagely
through the store's stacks like parallel raccoons. "See you in
an hour or so," my wife—my new girlfriend, then—said to
me, and as I watched her head to a dusty mass of surrealism, I
decided that this was the woman I was going to marry. About
six years later this was true, which is to say that my beautiful
romantic thought there in the bookstore was made true retro-
actively, when we walked down the synagogue aisle. They are
both lovely moments in my life, wandering away from my new
girlfriend in a bookstore, and listening to the organist playing,
who knows why, "How Do You Solve A Problem Like Maria?,"
a song from a musical featuring nuns and Nazis, at our Jewish
ceremony. The two moments feel connected—in fact, it feels
like each moment explains the other, which is why I tell the
bookstore story in the first place. But of course our marriage
is not sustained by the fact that we both wanted to shop separately that afternoon in Vermont. The story is not one that
illuminates our relationship, really—it is more a story to itself,
bright and sweet, that feels good to tell. I even liked writing
it down, and it made me go find a book I bought that day and
still own: *A Mirror for Witches*, a novel by Esther Forbes, a
Pulitzer Prize–winning author, largely forgotten. The book is
beautiful but weird, and its opening—

> It has long been known that, on occasions, devils in the shape of humanity or in their own shapes (that is, with horns, hoofs and tails) may fancy mortal women. By dark arts, sly promises of power, flattery, etc., they may prevail even upon Christian women, always to the destruction of these women's souls and often to that of their bodies.

—embodies the common notion that marriage is a trick—usually a less dramatic one than the devil and Christian women, but a trick nonetheless. In the novel of mine, marriage is something of a long con—literally, in the case of one of the marriages. A young woman snatches up a tech mogul as part of a plot for money, although whether the resulting marriage is less genuine or happy than that of a parallel couple, linked for love, is up to the reader.

My first puzzling marriage was, like many people's, that of my parents. It is not so much that their relationship is puzzling—it is really only as puzzling as anyone else's looks from the outside—but the marriage itself. Both of my parents insisted, for instance, both when questioned separately and together, that neither of them had ever proposed marriage, which made their union, in my mind, not so much a trick as a locked room mystery: they remained married for years and years—'til my father's death did them part—but had never had the idea to enter into it. Given how little grasp I had on their union, it is no surprise that I never asked them for any romantic or marital advice, and sure enough, despite giving advice on everything else, the only thing I remember my father telling me on such matters, when I was going out on a date, was that you can never go wrong telling your date they look beautiful, something which seemed dubious and sexist when I heard it but which worked, in my dating life, one hundred percent of the time. My mother told me once, dropping me off at a party, to remember that people liked to talk about themselves, which is perhaps the same piece of advice and has worked similar wonders, although as far as what that says about their marriage, I can't quite imagine. When I was eighteen, I learned that my mother had been married before—a thunderbolt for me at that age, but now her first husband, never met and long dead, just seems like a sidebar shrug, sort of like the woman who appeared at my father's funeral, an old girlfriend who seemed disappointed that no one had heard of her. Of course we hadn't.

The story of how my parents met is romantic enough—in that long-ago opera box. But that is all I know of the story. Their eyes met during the overture, they flirted at intermission over little plastic cups of champagne, and as the curtain rang down they concocted some story to share a cab—these are all things I am making up. Indeed, I once told a reporter how my parents met, and somehow what ended up in the newspaper is that my mother was an opera singer, something I still get asked about. (My mother taught the deaf, which is arguably sort of the opposite.) Someone else had filled in the blanks, even better than I could.

It is perhaps no surprise that a scene my mind turns to often, when I think of my parents' marriage, is not from their married life at all, but from a famous book. Every time I reread the book—from elementary school until today—I am startled once again to find this scene on the page, because I half remember it from my own life, with my own family at cocktail hour:

"That's the clumsiest dance I ever saw. Miss Berry assigned this?"

"Miss Berry assigned the onion part. I'M making up the DANCE," Harriet said pointedly.

"Oh," said Mrs. Welch discreetly.

Harriet fell over again, this time rolling away almost into the bathroom.

Mr. Welsch came into the room. "What's going on in here? It sounds like someone hitting a punching bag."

"She's being an onion."

They stood watching Harriet fall over and over again.

Mr. Welsch put his pipe in his mouth and crossed his arms. "According to Stanislavsky you have to feel like an onion. Do you feel like an onion?"

"Not in the least," said Harriet.

"Oh, come on. What are they teaching you in school these days?" Mrs. Welsch started to laugh.

"No, I'm serious. There's a whole school downtown that's probably rolling all over the floor right this minute."

"I never WANTED to be an onion," Harriet said from the floor.

"And it's a good thing. How many parts do you think are written for onions these days?" Mr. Welsch laughed. "I don't imagine you did want to be an onion. For that matter, who knows if an onion does either."

Mrs. Welsch laughed up at him. "You're so smart. Let's see *you* fall like an onion."

"Don't mind if I do," said Mr. Welsch, and putting down his pipe, he fell solidly to the floor. The floor shook.

"Honey! Did you hurt yourself?"

Mr. Welsch just lay there flat. "No," he said quietly, "but it's not as easy as it looks." He lay there breathing. Harriet took another fall just to keep him company.

"Why don't you get up, honey?" Mrs. Welsch stood over him with a worried look on her face.

"I'm trying to feel like an onion. The closest I can get is a scallion."

Harriet tried to feel like an onion. She found herself screwing her eyes up tight, wrapping her arms around her body, then buckling her knees and rolling to the ground.

"My God, Harriet, are you sick?" Mrs. Welsch rushed over to her.

Harriet rolled round and round the room. It wasn't bad at all, this being an onion. She bumped into her father, who started to laugh. She couldn't keep her face screwed up and laughed at him.

Her father started being an onion in earnest, rolling and rolling. Harriet suddenly jumped up and started to write in her notebook.

"The closest I can get is a scallion." This is something I can see my father saying—with the sort of certainty one has about a million memories ("I can see it like it was yesterday") accurate or not. In any case it didn't happen to my family at all. It happened in *Harriet the Spy* by Louise Fitzhugh, which is, with apologies to *Beloved, Moby Dick, Lolita, The Long Goodbye,* and *Time Will Darken It,* the Great American Novel. While this scene has some superficial similarities to my home life—I was raised by a heterosexual couple who were interested in my schooling and often up for some silliness in circumstances comfortable enough to roll around in—I think the reason for its loose-boundaried resonance in my mind is actually summarized in what comes next, what Harriet writes in her notebook:

I WONDER WHAT IT WOULD BE LIKE TO BE A TABLE OR A CHAIR OR A BATHTUB OR ANOTHER PERSON.

The sense of wonder, at all the blanks of the world, and the sense of invention, writing in a notebook to figure out in her own words, gets at the crucial heart of literature. It is a testament to the power of *Harriet the Spy* as a work of imagination that self-replicates. So many wonderful novels make me want to quit writing, because they're so wonderful. *Harriet the Spy*, on the other hand, inspires millions of people to become writers, even the vast majority of them who don't. For many young people, it's the first intoxicating sip of the brilliant stuff of dreaming things up. It's no wonder I snitched the scene to fill in a story I couldn't figure out all by myself.

For many years my parent's marriage confounded me as a unique mystery, but that's no longer the case. I've witnessed too many marriages begin, end, falter and endure, without understanding a whit of it, for my mother and father to be particularly puzzling. Traits or hobbies I can hardly endure for fifteen minutes have bound friends of mine in lasting bliss—bliss that's then halted, sometimes, leaving me wondering why that thing in particular was the last straw. I've been a spectator, sometimes too closely, for bouts of forgiveness and fighting over things I've found unforgivable and not worth mentioning, respectively, and my own marriage, twenty-six years at press date, is its own mystery, too.

We honeymooned in Paris, where I'd never been before, and spent a few days of it going over the proofreading for my first novel, the sort of thing we'd never do now but then seemed quite romantic. One of the characters in *The Basic Eight* turns out to be, perhaps, a figment of another character's imagination, and the proofreader had decided to put all mentions and actions of this character in brackets. We spent maybe three afternoons laying around the apartment we'd borrowed, taking turns writing *stet*—newly learned professional shorthand for *please leave this the way I wrote it*—in the margins of the manuscript. The rest of the time we wandered around the city, and what I remember most is feeling slightly indignant that no one had ever told me how beautiful Paris was, a ridiculous thing to think, like not having heard an elephant was big, or that love can make you happy.

There's a photograph I have from that time, framed on my desk, that has the odd luck of capturing a moment I genuinely remember. The picture was taken by a cousin of mine who said the sky was beautiful behind us—it was and it is—and I kissed my wife thinking that everything seemed beautiful. But of course this, along with "see you in an hour or so" and "how do you solve a problem like Maria?" is no more illustrative of our own marriage than "one should always be drunk" or "the closest I can get is a scallion." They're just the little glimpses, or whatever you might call them—whatever isn't the blanks you're filling in. My wife and I are very happy together—it is a floating happiness, a blurry mystery that slips between these anecdotes and moments.

This slipperiness is perhaps best expressed in one of my favorite books in the world, one I always want to slip into high school curricula. It is *The Pillow Book*, or anyway that's what most people call it, by Sei Shōnagon, a tenth-century Japanese noblewoman who wrote the book for herself. (A story goes that when a man found it and wanted to publish it, she was mortified, but as women in that era and locale were severely encouraged to be invisible, it's likely the story is more complicated than that.) It is not a novel, and it is not an account of her time. It is bits and pieces—lists, observations, anecdotes and other miscellany—notes that she took during idle hours. It is often said that these items form a portrait of Sei Shonagon and/or her era, and I suppose that's true, to an extent. But what is more alluring is what is missing. There's so much remembrance and so little self-reflection, so many opinions and so little conclusion, endless specifics that give us little general idea of someone we don't know and will never meet. *The Pillow Book* freezes a pile of captured moments without any framework to put them in—so the reader, inevitably, makes one up. The book invites participation, from a time and culture in which no one can participate anymore. Between each of Shonagon's short entries is space for the reader to decide which ones are important, emblematic or just worth thinking about for a little longer. "Everything that cries in the night is wonderful," goes a passage I often quote to new parents, "with the exception, of course, of babies," and once, in the middle of a professional dispute, I had this taped to my office wall: "*Things people despise—A crumbling earth wall. People who have a reputation for being exceptionally good-natured.*" It is a book that seems, with every reading, buoyed by joy or weighed down by unhappiness, frivolous or almost too deep for whatever afternoon I've picked it up again, concrete and historical or dizzyingly escapist. Because of its form and its faraway origins, *The Pillow Book* is an extreme example of a book that lets the reader make what hay they will, but all my favorite books have these gaps, these blanks that fit the little feelers of the reader's burrowy mind. It was something I was particularly aware of when composing *A Series of Unfortunate Events*, which is full of such blanks. While the Baudelaire orphans flee a mysterious villain and chase after a shuffle of inscrutable MacGuffins, there's a whole other story, of a secret organization and a distant female figure and, of course, of Mr. Snicket himself, as baffled as he is baffling in the world of the story. I've had to explain, to cranky literalist educators and dollar-eyed entertainment executives both, the importance of keeping such gaps, to remember that the central gambit of the reader's search for answers is the longing, not the answers, not only in literature, it seems to me—and here is where I generally lose the executives—but in life. And even if I could tell you exactly what underpins my happy marriage, or lay bare with dull certainty the secret workings of anyone else's, what joy would there be in that? Surely it is more fun, more essential, to stumble amidst the blanks we find in the world, understanding little but delighting in the resulting blur, free of all those tangible burdens which drive us, at least sometimes, to drink.

8

Do things have to mean things?

the Jack of Hearts and Queen of Spades converse
portentously of long-dead love-affairs.

Do things have to mean things? I can never decide. These lines
are from a big, long Baudelaire poem called "Spleen," and I
really like them. I like picturing two face cards talking to each
other, and "portentously" has a fortunetelling ring to it, which
seems appropriate and spookily enjoyable. Still, what does it
mean? I'm pretty sure I have no idea. When I read these lines,
the cards just bump my mind around, their conversation like
one you might hear at night between adults when you're a child
drifting off to sleep in another room. The actual words just feel
like a means to an end, a method or a tool, to take me to some
little card table in a corner of my consciousness. I like being
there. I'm not sure if I'm supposed to know why I've been led to
this card table, and I don't.

The poem is a section of *The Flowers of Evil* called "Spleen and Ideal," which outlines an enormous idea about our earthy, fleshy real selves and our lofty, impossible dreams of perfection. At least, I think it does. I never quite figure it out, but it sounds so cool, *Spleen and Ideal*, which is doubtless why it was swiped to title an album that roamed the dorms when I was in college. *Spleen and Ideal* by the arty, drony outfit Dead Can Dance is a classic make-out album, a genre in which the music itself stands back, in favor of mood and texture and effect, whether you're actually making out or just wishing you were: the martini-drenched longing of Roxy Music's *Avalon*, the seductive cool in Miles Davis's *Kind of Blue*, the Gregorian wallpaper of Enigma's *MCMXC a.D*, the spacey stasis of My Bloody Valentine's *Loveless*, the perhaps too-bluntly titled but nonetheless effective Marvin Gaye album, *Let's Get It On*. The quality of the music is irrelevant. The lyrics and melodies, the performance and production, whatever lofty ideals (or lack thereof) floating around the artists' heads all take a back seat to, well, getting it on in the back seat.

I like thinking about this space, in which the engagement and enjoyment of an art form is almost entirely detached from the stuff of the art itself. It makes me think of another album title, which, unlike *Spleen and Ideal*, I understand utterly: *Taking Drugs To Make Music To Take Drugs To*. The artist works hard doing a thing, and people—hopefully—find the thing and have some reaction to it. You might hope that the audience's state of mind matches the artist's—that is, that they're taking the same drug. But of course they hardly ever are. And even if they were, how in the world would you know?

In literature this space looms larger than it does in music. One can argue that Paul Chambers's loomy, foggy bass work on *Kind of Blue* is an intrinsic aspect of the album's lush, spare appeal, even if the undergraduates rolling around are hardly aware of it. But some of our most powerful experiences with literature happen when the words are hardly listened to, even subliminally. Consider being read to as a child, and the way your mind floated away from the story as you drifted off to sleep, or when the view out the window shapes the state of your mind more than the book read aloud in your headphones. The author has taken you someplace, but maybe wasn't driving the vehicle.

There is, in fact, a whole planet of literary appreciation that is only distantly orbiting the actual texts. People declare themselves in favor of Jeffersonian democracy, or label a situation Kafkaesque, who haven't read Jefferson or Kafka in years, or ever. Books are declared overrated, overlooked, major, minor, offensive and/or life-changing without being opened. Our shelves are full of mighty statements important to us that we haven't quite gotten around to yet, and books from distant schooldays whose sole purpose is to show we've read them, and sometimes—often—we haven't. "As Virginia Woolf wrote," someone said to me once, in a sentimental moment, "you can't go home again," and it would have been rude to point out that they meant Thomas Wolfe, because what difference does it make? I've read all 743 woolgathery but ultimately pleasurable pages of *You Can't Go Home Again*, and it does not put that ordinary but profound statement, a source of solace and wonder to so many who hear it, into sharper focus.

The space runs deeper than bragging and padding. Literature

has a mythology attached to it, a noble and highfalutin position attractive to adherents and enemies alike. There is an enduring image of a writer, untethered to the practice of writing, because it's hardly tethered to anything: someone financially success-ful who lives in a garret, spending all day yanking pages out of a typewriter, or hunching over parchment with a shivering plume (never, say, a laptop) only to emerge into prominence with work so startling and new that it greatly upsets an establish-ment who nevertheless welcomes them with open arms. People who hardly read books clamor for contracts to write them—the better to be part of a literary idea with principles they respect and admire without quite knowing what they are. A universally loved rebel, an immensely popular loner, the imaginary writer is everyone's favorite, if only because you don't have to read any-thing to appreciate their work, although I must say I prefer their earlier stuff.

This myth is at its most free and radiant in poetry. The imagi-nary image of a poet is so hazy as to be almost invisible. Attempts to codify it, with, say, a quill pen or a black turtleneck, have proved futile. Being a poet is very vague—anyone can imagine themselves as one, so it's no wonder just about everyone tries. There may be some rare examples of writers who begin writing essays or fiction sui generis, some playwrights and screenwriters whose first creative scrawl was "Scene One," but nearly every-one begins with poetry. Whether you ever wrote again or not, you've scrawled a few lines someplace, perhaps from untouched imagination but more likely in imitation of something, a school assignment or a glimpse someplace of words arranged unusu-ally, some snippet overheard that was performative and striking.

There was something alluring about writing—that's why you did it—but also the idea of writing. By the time adolescence hit, you might have had some idea of being a poet, utterly separate from any delight you might have had writing poetry. There are some people who seem to write solely in imitation of this glamorous image of their profession, throughout their lengthy, tedious careers. But we all do it when we start. The myth of poetry justifies this compulsion so many of us have to write things down anyway. We know, however dimly, that what we're writing down are just little scraps, of interest to no one, hardly even ourselves. But that's when the mythology beckons, offering the idea that these crappy scraps are superior and vital and magic. They aren't just scraps—they mean something. They're an Ideal, not just a Spleen, or maybe it's the other way around.

Like countless others I started writing little poems who knows when, and by middle school I was thoroughly entranced by the idea that writing poems made me thoroughly entrancing. I longed to be tormented—not in the various ways, large and small, that my adolescence was actually tormenting, but in some glamorous, mythical way, just like I kept writing poetry whilst longing to be a real poet, the kind who could get away with the word *whilst*. I wrote poems for love objects I was only sort of interested in, and poems describing the natural world, which I found too gritty and itchy whenever I actually went out in it. I remember winning a little prize for young local poets, awarded to my sad elegy about San Francisco's cable cars, which were briefly taken out of circulation for repair and refurbishment. I hardly ever rode the cable cars and can't imagine I felt any emotion whatsoever about the short interruption of service.

I just felt it was the thing to write about. I can't find this poem, unfortunately—all I remember is that several lines begin with a word that is ordinary and conversational unless you spell it without the *h*, rendering it epic and tormented: *O!*

Fun as it is to sneer at my teenage self, there was something very genuine about what it was I was trying to do, which sat alongside the performative torment like parallel play. I kept trying to make my terrible poems less so. I was as taken with actual literature as I was with its mythos, or, to put it another way, I thought Baudelaire was cool but also kept reading him. Slowly, I moved away from the thought that poetry needed to express things dramatically and heroically—*O! Cable cars!*—to something a little more difficult to describe but easier to love. I got interested in this kind of juxtaposition, the way words and phrases could sit on the page and influence each other and the reader, without making exact strict sense. This was not only happening in Baudelaire; it was everywhere around me. There was a stanza—if stanza's what you call it—from a hit song by the band New Order that was always rolling around in my mind:

> I see a ship in the harbor
> I can and shall obey
> But if it wasn't for your misfortunes
> I'd be a heavenly person today

The way the lines all add up to something—longing, discontent, maybe some dramatic or even sordid backstory—really struck me, even if I didn't quite know what it meant. I did know that New Order was a band who rose from the ashes of another band called Joy Division, after their lead singer, the hypnotic Ian Curtis, had killed himself. All of their music seemed in sad tribute to this tragedy: the music was perfectly formed, often mechanical in nature, but the vocals and the lyrics were rough and fragmentary, mourning the space where Curtis would have been. The songs weren't necessarily *about* their dead friend, but invoked him nonetheless, through the resonant slippage of the words. They mourned to make music to make me feel mournful.

There's not enough absinthe in my house—and there's a lot of absinthe in my house—for me to reproduce my high school poetry here for gapes and giggles. Of course it wasn't good. I had decided it didn't necessarily have to mean anything, which meant that it was misunderstood by the precious few who read it. A classmate showed romantic interest in me, for instance, but we were from vastly irreconcilable worlds, i.e., two years apart. The best thing to do, obviously, was to kiss her and then write her a long, obscure poem explaining why a relationship was impossible. When she continued to show interest, my friend had to sit me down and explain, doing her best, I'm sure, to keep her eyes from rolling back into her head. "Daniel, it doesn't matter what the poem says," she told me, after school in the middle courtyard, "you wrote her a *poem*," and the thrill of being so thoroughly misread—I mean, of course, the despair of it—led me to write even more melancholic verse. I was in an infinite loop, taking drugs to make music to take drugs to make music to take drugs to—until the woman in question realized that I was not so much suffering as insufferable.

I brought some of these poems to college, along with a print of Klimt's *The Kiss* and several make-out albums on cassette, but when I submitted them to the college literary magazine they were openly mocked. They didn't *mean* anything. (Critiques were anonymous, though I'm sure my silent, flushed presence surely gave my colleagues a clue as to who this dreadful poet was.) I got the message: things had to mean things now. Literature was not some arty pretense, of course it wasn't, but it wasn't just a luxuriant pleasure either. We weren't in high school anymore—that was a year or so ago. I was an adult now, taking classes on Shakespeare and British modernism and the Harlem Renaissance and Vladimir Nabokov, analyzing and deconstructing—deconstructing was the big thing—texts in serious ways. If the words were still sometimes confusing, one only had to talk about the form being used, the culture that the artist was from, or—tut, tut—not from. There were clear, academic earmarks of reading books properly, and, well, if by chance we found any of this literature inspiring, we were to pursue that privately, on our own time.

I did. Though it seemed in some ways antithetical to the way literature was being discussed in class, I kept trying to make some, by writing little scraps of things stuck in my head, in an order that felt compelling to me. Little scraps enshrined in the mind, presented on a table in a conscious order, is as good a definition of literature as any, but compared to the lofty halo of literature as it was studied, mine felt like a dirty habit. I lived in a shared household self-righteous about the environment, so I wrote poems on the backs of graded essays, student bulletins, even take-out menus with space in the margins, so as not to waste paper. Strict poetic forms were attractive to me, and made poetry less of a dubious pose and more of a parlor game.

If you had something to start with, you didn't need to rely on pure inspiration, which sometimes showed up and sometimes didn't. I still find this kind of structure very handy; my novels all have a framework that was comforting on days when my sentences are turning out gray and lumpy. I've used the form of a diary, an opera, a twelve-step program, a parlor game; chapters in novels mirror one another, or correspond with illustrations by a collaborator; they've mimicked the order of pop songs on an album I like, or formed a tradition of their own—a sequence of thirteen novels, for instance, each with thirteen chapters and a single coda. When my writing day begins, I know what to do next, even when I do it badly.

When I was writing poetry, the form that was most appealing was the sestina, which has six six-line stanzas, in which the ending words of each line are all the same but rotated in a specific order. The sestina has been used for ages and practiced by all sorts of poets, but the one that struck me was one that strikes a lot of people, "Sestina" by Elizabeth Bishop, an American poet who might be my favorite. It begins like this:

> September rain falls on the house.
> In the failing light, the old grandmother
> sits in the kitchen with the child
> beside the Little Marvel Stove,
> reading the jokes from the almanac,
> laughing and talking to hide her tears.

The ending words—*house, grandmother, child, stove, almanac, tears*—hover around the rest of the poem, which stays, almost necessarily, there in the kitchen, the recurrence of the people and objects both comforting and insular. A sestina has a three-line stanza at the end called the envoi, in which all six words must appear. Bishop's envoi was something I could not stop staring at:

> Time to plant tears, says the almanac.
> The grandmother sings to the marvelous stove
> And the child draws another inscrutable house.

It's not unlike Baudelaire's playing card conversation, startling and resonant but with a specific, fixed meaning unclear—in fact, in poetry like this, the meaning of "meaning" becomes a little unclear. It's not as if we don't know what's going on in these lines. Even the less literal language—the almanac saying something, the stove being marvelous—is not at all confusing. What's unclear, perhaps, is why Bishop is saying these things. But that is not really confusing either—she is describing a scene, perhaps from memory, because she is thinking about it, and she wants us to think about it, too. She's taking drugs to make music to take drugs to.

I pursued this where it went. I wrote a lot of sestinas and then invented little forms of my own, nothing obvious to the reader but clear and useful to me, so composing lines felt like laying tinsel on top of a tree. My poetry got better—which would almost have to be the case—and instead of treasuring the fact that I was a poet while writing things that seemed mythically poetic, I treasured writing. I kept using Bishop as a guide, which is a double-edged sword, because her clear, deceptively straightforward work makes good company but is very hard to get good at. Even when she seems to lack for inspiration, her poetry makes magic, as in "Twelve O'clock News," a poem about the mess on her desk, with stanzas under individual headings—"typewriter," "envelopes," etc. It opens with "Goose-Neck Lamp":

> As you all know, tonight is the night of the full moon, half the world over. But here the moon seems to hang motionless in the sky. It gives very little light; it could be dead. Visibility is poor. Nevertheless, we shall try to give you some idea of the lay of the land and the present situation.

That quiet, still tone was very interesting to me, along with the form: little headlines and full sentences, the language ordinary but cryptic, creating a nice distance from the banal subject matter. I tried to do it myself, in a poem called "The Apple Interviews," in which different kinds of apples, ripening on my rented windowsill, try to explain themselves, and the poet teaching my poetry-writing class had me stay after one day, to tell me, very gently, that perhaps I was practicing another literary tradition, that of prose, which surely I had heard of and at which it was far more possible, though still not likely, to make a living.

It was a little ill-timed, this advice. I'd just won a contest, and I was spending a few evenings with the other Connecticut Student Poets, giving readings at other campuses, trying not to fall asleep at the wheel on my way back late at night. The car was on loan from the university—something that seems like a reckless liability, now that I think about it—and the radio didn't work. To stay awake I told myself stories—aloud, like a

parent at a child's bedtime, or like a person at a party. The stories were in prose, I guess you'd say, and I began to think that
maybe my poetry teacher was right. For years, I'd thought that
I would write novels, but that was mostly more mythmaking—
the idea of being a novelist was very sexy, but here I was twenty
years old and I hadn't written one yet, so it might have been too
late. And didn't novels have to be about enormous, significant
things? After all, the classics I was reading in my classes were
merely springboards for talking about powerful, vague ideas we
all at least pretended to understand. But a powerful, vague idea
was forming in my own mind, that perhaps what I was trying to
do in poetry, something clear but indirect, imaginative but not
deliberately obscure, had a word already. The word was *story*,
the thing I kept muttering on the highway, something which
on one level merely described, in an interesting way, what was
going on, but also made you think about something else, led you
to feel some way not just about the world of the story, about the
actual world you were in, reading. I wasn't good at it—I knew
this even then—but it seemed like a good thing to do. This was
a real revelation to me—finding a location for literature in my
mind that was neither pretension nor deconstruction, something that doesn't ignore the text in favor of mythmaking or
paint over it with academic analysis, a space in which I could try
to think about things so that other people might think about
them, too.

I can remember the moment this idea really sunk in—I was
leaving my Nabokov class, taught by the professor whom I'd later
run into outside the hospital. She remains dear to my heart, but
while I loved reading Nabokov's gossamer and sharp-toothed

prose, his terrifyingly erudite brain meant that we spent a lot of time in class examining his wide-ranging literary references and other rhetorical puzzles, which was not always what I wanted to be doing while reading him. It felt a little like capturing butter-flies and pinning them down, but, as any Nabokov fan knows, that guy loved capturing butterflies and pinning them down, so I tried to be a good sport.

That day we were discussing *Pnin*, a comic novel of his which takes place on a college campus not unlike the campus where Nabokov taught, or the campus where I was studying him. *Pnin* is one of my favorite books in the world. It is often described as a comic novel, although its tone might be more accurately described as awkward. The titular hero, an awkward man, fails and fails again, in a sequence of anecdotes of increasing hilarity. But this increasing hilarity is sad, too—the more time we spend with the bumbly Pnin, the crueler it feels to laugh at him, and the more ashamed we are of finding him comic. This contradiction—which is itself both funny and sad—was what I was liking about the novel, along with a luminous scene involving a glass bowl which I don't want to spoil. Instead, my class had been discussing one of the book's motifs, the regular appearance of squirrels—toy squirrels, squirrels on postcards, even a pair of squirrel-fur shoes, along with squirrels scamper-ing around campus and generally acting squirrely. What all these squirrels meant was the question of the day—they must have meant something—and we all proffered theories, rang-ing from Aesop (of course not) to colonialism (now we're on to something), until it was time to go. I left the building and there was a squirrel—then another, then a couple more, crossing my path on their way to various trees. *Oh*, I thought, not *O!* but *Oh*. I realized that Nabokov, crossing campus and pondering his novel, must have seen squirrels, too, and now, having read and thought about them, here I was staring at them, too. My lengthy gaze made me feel like I was on drugs, but there was no way of knowing if Nabokov was taking the same stuff. Nabokov might have meant something specific with these squirrels, but he wasn't here. It was just me, staring at squirrels not because of Aesop or colonialism but because there they were, squirrels.

From there my mind went to a poem I had on my desk by Lorine Niedecker, a new discovery of mine, whose ordinary inscrutability, not dissimilar from Bishop's, was leading me toward the sentences I wanted to write:

> A monster owl
> out on the fence
> flew away. What
> is it the sign
> of? The sign of
> an owl.

The sign of an owl, the sign of a squirrel, the sign of the writing I was reading and the writer I wanted to be. This idea, both obvious and obscure, grounded me, both the lack of precious meaning in the words and the soaring feeling they gave me. I kept pursuing, keep pursuing, both of these things, the undeniable physicality of what I like to read and the supernatural, invisible effect that it has—the spleen, in other words, and the ideal. Whatever that means.

9

This is what it sounds like.

Once, visiting a school to talk about my work, I stood in the hallway looking at some assignments on display, including a unit on literary devices. Among the metaphors and alliterations was a list students had been asked to make of euphemisms for various phrases including, I had to blink twice to see it, *poor people*. The kids tried their best. *Disadvantaged*, was one. *Underprivileged. Destitute.* I first wondered who on Earth would assign such a thing, and then, as I kept reading the students' attempts—*lower class, paupers, downtrodden, homeless*—I began instead to wonder what a euphemism was, exactly. I'd learned, long ago at some other school, that it was a sort of substitute, a gentler way, rather than the proper way, of saying something. But of course "poor people" is not a proper way of saying anything, however ungentle it might be. It seemed like a terrible example to bring into a classroom, although, as I stood there thinking of other topics for which we use euphemisms, I thought it was perhaps the safest choice. There aren't euphemisms for eating breakfast, or for tying your shoes—only for topics in some way unspeakable. But of course even the most explicit term for something is just a layer of words on some actual event, and in fact its explicitness only became unacceptable because we decided that the word for the thing shouldn't be the word for the thing. I felt all language fall away from me there in the hallway, and then the door opened and it was time to talk about literature. Because sometimes you have to say something.

> What will you say tonight, poor lonesome soul?
> What will you say, old withered heart of mine,
> to her, most good, most dear, most beautiful,
> beneath whose sacred eyes you bloom again?

Of all the Baudelaire skulking around my brain, that first line, "What will you say tonight?" is the one that refuses to leave. The whole poem is a prostration to Ideal Beauty as personified by a woman who isn't giving Baudelaire enough attention, a frequent subject in *The Flowers of Evil* which wears out its welcome about as quickly as Baudelaire likely did with the woman in question. That one question, though, floats free of all that. Its framing has a poignancy all its own, or maybe this is just because I've carried it so long. I used to think it to myself before a date, or a party—*what will you say tonight?*—but over the years it's become emblematic of any moment of suspense or hesitancy: a tense news day, a looming tempest in a teacup nearby, the sigh before a difficult conversation, a blank page waiting for me to do my job.

I remember the line ringing in my head in high school, when

I had to deliver terrible news. A classmate of mine, someone I scarcely knew, had died suddenly, and at school the news was travelling quickly, along with a countering rumor that he was alive and well and the subject of ghastly lies. As a result his friends were in a frenzy, and many of them were gathered for a rehearsal of which I was supposedly in charge. A teacher confirmed his death to me and then said I should make the announcement, which he presented as a leadership obligation but which I recognized even then as his being afraid to do it himself. *What will you say tonight*, I thought to myself, and then I told people their friend was dead. I said it just like that; I said his name and I said he was dead, and the room erupted in grief. Several people, including the teacher, told me I shouldn't have said it the way I did, and I still spend lost hours trying to think what the better way must have been—searching for some euphemism, maybe, that would rendered the death of a 17 year old easier to bear.

I always thought it was good to just say things. I think I learned this from Prince. Universally and properly understood to be a titan and a genius, Prince needs no cheerleading from me. But it is useful to be reminded that he was not universally recognized as such at the time when I first encountered him. I was in middle school and my friend bought an album of his that was a couple of years old, *Dirty Mind*, and we'd sit listening and staring at the cover. Prince looked ugly and creepy there, the titles of the songs spray-painted on the wall over his bed where he sprawled half-dressed, which is to say half-naked. I'd seen women depicted like this in rock and roll, but never a man, not that he looked exactly like a man or that what he played was exactly rock and roll. The song "Dirty Mind," for instance, had plenty of guitar, but underneath was an electronic pulse, not so much a beat as a throb. Lots of musicians were using electronic drums then, and their mannered sounds were often used to create a stark, numbing distance from humanity, backing a philosophical, sometimes pretentious bent to the lyrics: *I can't understand what makes a man hate another man, when people run in circles it's a very mad world.* I liked this stuff, but Prince was different. The electronics didn't sound intellectual, but actual—like cheap cordless phones, or the warning buzzers of automobiles—and the lyrics were forthright and direct, an antidote to the aspirational dreams and philosophical flightiness of the other stuff. *Explicit,* was the word I learned for it, the x in the word a little unsettling, just like Prince saying he had a dirty mind. It was so bracing it took me a couple of years to even know I liked it.

By then Prince was a huge star, understood to be very good-looking, and courting notoriety for his explicit eroticism. This was certainly part of his style, but for me Prince was also explicit in the way he had first struck me—telling me something more directly than anyone else on the stereo. The song I liked best told me that if I didn't like the world I was living in, to take a look around; at least I had friends. This was true, and it was a kind of reassurance, solid as a guardrail, that so many other songs seemed too flighty to offer. Love songs, given stumbling attempts at early romance, seemed like castles in the clouds, but they would play Prince at a dance, and I would look around; at least I had friends. They could die at any moment, but now they were here in the gymnasium, actually, sweatily, explicitly.

In another way, though, Prince was anything but explicit. As with so many canonized artists, it can sometimes take a moment to realize how inexplicable they really are. For some context, two other huge pop stars of this time were Bruce Springsteen, whose big hit song chronicled the pride and shame of a veteran born in the USA, and Madonna, whose big hit song was about feeling so rejuvenated from a romantic relationship that she felt like a virgin. Patriotic ballads and dewy love songs are fairly traditional song topics. Prince's big song, on the other hand, compared a relationship, possibly imaginary but certainly dysfunctional, to the sound of doves crying. Even this makes it sound more sensible than it is, because the comparison is made in a slippery lyric. "This is what it sounds like when doves cry," the chorus says, but the antecedent for *this* isn't clear. It could be the relationship, or the music itself: *this* is what it sounds like. My school tried briefly to ban the playing of Prince's music, thus guaranteeing his enduring popularity with the student body, but although there is plenty of Prince content that can easily enrage those waiting to be offended, there is something unexpressed, something implicit, about his explicitness, that makes people want to ban him even when he isn't saying anything. He rolls his eyes, he licks his lips, he dares you to think about what he knows you know he is thinking about. Far more often than he was dirty, he had a dirty mind.

The way the explicit and the unexpressed are so much closer to each other than we might think, and both equally distant from whatever it is we think we mean, is something that began to guide me in my own expression, and lack thereof, on the page. Like most writers, I have an impulse to be a truthteller. Each book I write fills a gap I see in the literary landscape, even if I'm the only one who can see it—something nobody's quite said before in quite that way. But they're novels, not manifesti, and even when their stories and ideas address the real world, the books aren't realistic—more often than not, they're fantastical. But the fantastical elements feel, to me, like the cleanest way to tell the plain truth. An indictment of this world we've made, which treats children cruelly in every sphere, is not nearly as interesting, as readable, as three orphans being thrown down an elevator shaft in *The Ersatz Elevator*; an extended metaphor linking the nerve-wracking pendulum of romantic attention with geological catastrophe is less compelling, in my mind, than various lovers trying to escape a volcano in *Adverbs*. The stories aren't true, but they rhyme with truth, they call up the truth the way a gentler term does with its uglier synonym. The explicit and the euphemistic end up sounding like each other.

Some years ago I was asked to speak on a panel about getting boys to read, an intermittent concern among educators and librarians. (The statistics are a little shaky, but there is an ongoing sense that boys lag behind girls in literacy.) The panel took place at a librarian conference I was attending anyway, to accept an award for *Why We Broke Up*. I'd toured extensively for that book, and for the first time there'd been a visible gender discrepancy in my audiences. Previously, it had always seemed about 50-50; for this book there seemed to be far more young women than young men. The book was being received as a romance, which wasn't too surprising, and neither was it a problem—different people like different books—but it was interesting to me to visit a high school and see, for the first time, a slant to who seemed most interested. I wondered, given this, what I might say at the panel, and then in a tidy coincidence, my mother was cleaning house and gave me a stack of books from my old bedroom: books I'd read and loved in high school, just when I was exactly the sort of young man missing from my own book tour.

It was a funny stack, curated by my own teenage pretension and delight, guided a bit by some publishing trends of the 1980s and whatever other mysterious methods brought culture to young people, forever lost to the internet. (I'm pretty sure I read Balzac's *Lost Illusions*, for instance, because the author's name is mentioned disapprovingly by the prudish ladies in *The Music Man*—a seven-hundred page commitment prompted by a two-second gag.) Both high and low culture were represented; there were books by men and women, contemporary authors and ones from bygone eras, literature in English and literature in translation, books I still loved and books I could no longer stand. Also, lots and lots and lots of sex scenes. Milan Kundera's *The Unbearable Lightness of Being*, for example, remained a luminous meditation on life's fleetingness, set against the 1968 invasion of Czechoslovakia—and also has all the juicy details of our hero's voluminous sex life. William Wiser's *Disappearances* chronicled Paris in the 1920s, but I'd forgotten the narrator's obsessions included not just Picasso and the Bluebeard murder case, but a lithe young prostitute up for anything. Oscar Hijuelos's *The Mambo Kings Play Songs of Love* was the passionate immigration story I'd kept in my head—and it contained more oral sex per page than any other novel I've encountered.

These books were what fascinated and moved me at that age, as literature began to lead me down the path of my adult life. But it was clear, rereading them then, that part of what fascinated and moved me was their explicitness—not much of a surprise, really, for a teenager. And explicit content, of course, is what is policed the most in literature for young people. The most-banned books, a list updated yearly in America, are invariably banned for sexuality—and those were the books the publishers had already vetted for such an audience. It became clear what might be interesting to say on a panel for people simultaneously interested in bringing more adolescent boys to literature and blocking access to the subject matter known to particularly interest that same slice of the population.

I began my talk by reading aloud, without preamble, a long erotic passage from the Hijuelos novel—my favorite sentence was "They seemed to love each other so much, their skin gave off a lustful heat and smell so strong that they would attract packs of wild hounds who'd follow them down the streets"—and then I explained what it was: A Pulitzer Prize–winning book, recalling the triumphs and scrapes of a Cuban musician making his way in America, the prose lively and inventive, critiquing identity and popular culture in ways both thoughtful and relevant, including a consideration of the drives and damages of masculinity—just what you'd want a young man to read, except that it had dirty parts, so it would never be offered to such a reader, who would instead be led toward, for example, a current hit YA series about teenagers murdering each other in a dystopic arena. It was time, I said, to reconsider the types of literature we were offering an audience that might be hungry for something else.

I thought it went pretty well. There was a reception that evening, where several librarians said I should publish the list of the books I'd reread, and any other explicit titles that came to mind. I thought a better idea was to write one myself. Fresh from accepting a prize for *Why We Broke Up*, I began to think about another book for young readers, though perhaps more likely to appeal to more genders. I already had the spark of an idea, also collected on tour, from another school visit.

I was going to speak in the gymnasium, and while the audience filed in, I was "backstage," that is, in an adjoining classroom dedicated to sex ed. (Why do the gym teachers so often teach about sex? Is it because both activities are sweaty?) On the teacher's desk was a box in which students could submit anonymous questions. Of course I read them, and one of them asked why it was perfectly acceptable to ask a girl for a massage if your neck or arm were stiff, but not to ask for other quick forms of physical relief. Then it was time to talk about the romance I'd written, and as I discussed *Why We Broke Up* to another largely female audience, every element of the anonymous question kept haunting me: the entitlement, the false equivalency, the most-likely-purposeful provocation, but also the sort of innocent sense of a mind trying to reduce sex to mere physical functionality—that is, just the way the gym teachers so often teach it. The policing of sexual content began to seem larger than an issue of making some literature ring hollow to a certain readership, or having books hidden from that readership, but part of a general puritanism that you could see manifesting itself in inquisitive young men. *What will you say tonight*, I asked myself, wondering what Prince would do. I started to think about the sort of young man, found in every high school, promiscuous or at least trying for promiscuity, whose blunt interest in sex was clear whether people found it troubling or exciting. An explicit boy, in other words.

It took me some time to find the right way into this story. My two other novels set in high school, *The Basic Eight* and *Why We Broke Up*, are in the forms of a diary and a long letter respectively, allowing for the digressive impulses of young narrators, who, like most young narrators, bear a bookish, introspective resemblance to the authors who dreamed them up. But this young man—Cole, named after a street near my house, where I sat in a café thinking this over—was a different sort of creature. He had a dirty mind. Not privy to thinking things through, he lived in a world lit by the handy ellipses of texting and by the short jolts of easy-access porn. As usual, I turned to my bookshelves for help, and lit upon one of my favorite novels in the world.

Why Did I Ever by Mary Robison takes the form of 536 little sections, some scarcely longer than a few words, from the point of view of a woman who is similarly scattered, troubled and jokey:

> "In my head," I tell him, "are the works of John Philip Sousa. And so loud that at first I thought the high school's band was practicing. I went and checked outside. I don't even know the words to 'It's a Grand Old Flag.'
>
> "Oh, come on," says he. "It's a grand old flag, dunt dunt high-flying flag. Dunt dunt duh, dunt dunt duh, dunt dunt duhhh."

The portrait that emerges, as both the plot and tone keep start-stopping, is similarly blaring and elusive, as the heroine gives us everything on her mind at the moment, and hardly anything between the large gaps of time and sense. Thus prompted, I began to write, on individual index cards, little bouts of Cole's thoughts and deeds, explicit and detached from anything but sex—*All the Dirty Parts*, was the title my wife gave to me:

> I taught Alana how to skip rocks, with my hand over her hand with the stone in it, like that. Also on a park bench, dark without wind kicking dirt on us, I taught her to make me come, basically the same way. You're getting the hang of it. You're a natural.

The book charts the path of a promiscuous boy whose explorations lead him to another boy, and then a girl, the complications piling up in the language of his own panting distraction. It was fun to move the cards around into different arrangements on my dining room table, and as the novel neared completion, I imagined that the gatekeepers of children's literature, who had not only awarded me a prize but had applauded my sex talk at the conference, would welcome such a book, and protect it from its inevitable detractors.

Wrong, wrong, wrong. The publishers of my books for young people hemmed and hawed, saluted my bravery and then admitted they were too scared to put it out. Luckily my adult publisher was happy to send such a book into the world, and although this meant that young people would have to find it for their own, I got busy promoting it, including publishing an essay cribbed from my presentation to the librarians. The editor of a leading children's literature journal pronounced the essay "bullshit," but I began to hear from enthusiastic readers—librarians and parents who were passing the book around, and from young people who were quietly appreciative. I had never received anonymous fan mail before, but it felt good to read that some readers felt "seen," as one high schooler put it, even if they did not want to be seen saying it.

I heard, too, from a librarian who'd been at the conference, declaring that my reading of the Hijuelos passage more than six years previously had been predatory toward the audience—which she accurately though curiously described as "majority female"—and to boys, too. "Do some work, fix that," she said to me, although of course she didn't really say this to me, but onscreen, publicly, where such ire was sure to spread. Spread it did, with a handful of other librarians popping up in a comments section to remember other remarks I'd made that they'd found objectionable. Within a week, I'd heard from my son's school, which had received repeated phone calls by someone wanting to tell him, given what they'd read online, that he was likely a child of rape—all presumably in opposition to my being explicit. It certainly worked. When I speak publicly now, it echoes even more in my mind: *What will you say tonight?*

My impulse, years later, is to write the names of such people here. Along with other children's writers similarly stung, I have kept an occasional eye on this particular group from my own screen, watching them condemn one book or another, calling for apologies, withdrawals, edits and revocations, interspersed with admonitions for a more inclusive community, and wondering why some young people, about whom they care very fervently—and I do believe this—aren't reading what they want them to read. It is tempting to be explicit about who they are, in the same way they were explicit about me. But condemnations of such censorship always feel melodramatic—too many authors can't wait to join the ranks of wronged artists by shushing the people who dare to shush them. Besides, as gatekeepers are always eager to remind us, it's not really censorship, anyway. *All the Dirty Parts* isn't confiscated and burned but widely available; following the L'Affaire Hijuelos, I had a few speaking invitations rescinded—including, hilariously, a panel on banning books—but such blacklisting is not censorship, either, any more than their continued objections and demands to writers and publishers is censorship. It explicitly isn't; of course it isn't. It just sort of rhymes with censorship. This is what it sounds like.

The most pernicious aspect of this accusatory corner of the discourse is that it leads people to censor themselves, ahead of the pearl-clutchers. There are many things I can't say in this book—many stories I cut from the manuscript or couldn't even bring myself to put into draft. Most of them aren't missed—they're redundant, or hopelessly obscure, things that have stuck in my mind for no discernible reason and have no discernible interest to others, and these I really stopped writing after just a couple of sentences, the way I try to do in conversation, when I suddenly realize I'm boring. But there are things I can't believe I'm not going to say. They would be better off said, is my instinct—things that make me look admirable and things that make me look horrid, secrets that seem wrong to keep and records that beg, glaringly, to be corrected. Such things would betray people's confidences, expectations, and comforts, things that reveal generosities and monstrosities from people visible and obscure. I can't tell if my self-censorship is discretion or cowardice—or just the dull truth that you simply can't say everything. Hardly any book is too short, I tell myself when I'm revising, as my pen hesitates over some drafted passage. And then I usually X it out. I tell myself I am thinking of my readers, but really I am thinking of someone else—my wife's grandmother.

Many years ago, my wife and I were in Miami, Florida, for a book festival, and were then going to drive about an hour to where her grandmother was living. It was before our phones told us how to get everywhere, so her grandmother took it upon herself to write out some directions for the drive. The resulting document is now a prized family heirloom. The directions are four pages long, not including a smaller, two-page supplement. There are three maps. The directions specify which lane to use, predictions about traffic, reminders about what change to have handy for tolls, and more than a few digressions about what roads *not* to use, as well as her take on the general state of driving culture in Delray Beach and the surrounding areas. It's a mass of overstatement and convolution, a *Tristram Shandy* of local logistics, explicit in a way neither Prince nor Baudelaire can touch. I think of it often, not just as a reminder of the perils of overwriting, but as a metaphor, or perhaps a euphemism, for the trip we're all on. Surrounded by so much nonsense, it can be tricky to find the explicit path you want, amidst all of the details you're missing, all the stories in which you don't get to participate. Everything is around you, but you can't take it all in and you certainly can't convey all of it to anyone who might be patient enough to listen to you. What do you censor, what do you keep? What will you say tonight? You can't say everything. But take a look around.

10

Alone on the bus.

The bus I take home is an obscure one. It goes right from my home to several places I like to be, and back again, and hardly anywhere else. It is not a popular bus, by which I mean not very many people take it, not that nobody likes it. In fact, everyone likes it, because it is never crowded—that is, it is popular because it is unpopular. It is at its emptiest as it approaches my house, because a couple stops beforehand, a bunch of people exit the bus to go to their condos in a building that used to be a hospital. Not only that, but it played a hospital in the movie *Vertigo*. My bus reaches the stop, and most or even all of the other passengers file off, and I get to think of Barbara Bel Geddes, who sits with silent, shell-shocked Jimmy Stewart after he's watched Kim Novak plunge to her supposed death. She realizes he's a hopeless case, and slowly, beautifully shot, she walks down the long hospital hallway and leaves the movie. We never see her again, and we in the audience have no idea how the rest of the movie will go. This is an idea that I stole for my novel

Watch Your Mouth—after a horrific event at a funeral halfway through, I wanted readers to have absolutely no idea what would happen next—*and then? And then? What else?* "That's why I was screaming," my narrator tells us, perhaps too dramatically, "because I knew it *wasn't* over, just as you, reading this, can feel the thick weight of unread book in your right hand . . . *More? How can there be more? How can there be a second part?*"

One afternoon I was the only passenger left. But the driver hadn't seen me, and as we pulled away from the *Vertigo* hospital, he began to sing, very loudly and proudly,

I'm alone on the bus!
I'm alone on the bus!

This song has loomed large. I am a big believer in, and performer of, the spur-of-the-moment self-composed song. My sister and I compete aloud in this art form whenever we are together and something unusual or something unremarkable or nothing happens, to the unconfirmed delight of our families. However, in this instance I was afraid the driver would skip my stop, so I had to pull the Stop Request cord, which rang its little reminder that he was, contrary to his performance, not alone on the bus. He took it pretty well. There was nothing to be self-conscious about, really; we both knew why he was singing. He was bored. That's the reason everyone sings, isn't it? The entire history of music, of any art-making actually, not to mention additional whole swaths of culture, even bits that seem utterly irreplaceable, sprung up for want of something to do. *It's a dull day,* I can picture some way-way-back ancestor sighing. *I think I'll hum something, or create antibiotics.*

No, no—this can't be it. Surely all artistic output stems from something a little nobler than boredom. It's why I like to dress it up and say *ennui* instead, to mean another kind of boredom, a French kind, more glamorous, better somehow, less blandly fidgety and more beautifully empty. But maybe ennui and boredom are the same thing. There's no other French term for boredom, so ennui and boredom can't really be different, the way fromage is not a better kind of cheese. So maybe the French are just bored differently. Certainly it seems like the French would think of it that way. Certainly it seems like Americans would think that the French would think of it that way, and the cheese, let's face it, is better in France.

Sometimes, at a library or bookstore where I have come to talk about my work, children will complain to me about being bored as they wait in line to meet me. I encourage them, instead, to say they are experiencing ennui. A young person who announces that a long car ride or twenty minutes in a waiting room is ennuyé (the obscure adjective form) seems to me more likely to find themselves entertained. It has an element of glamor, but something else, too—a sort of loneliness. A child is bored; you have to reach adolescence, and maybe stay there forever, to experience ennui.

When I was fourteen I went to a party—my first high school party. I did not really want to go, because I felt I had been invited out of pity—the hostess was a year or so older than me, the daughter of some family friends—and because I was afraid the party would be boring. It was. The music was boring—Jimmy Buffet, I think—and people stood in clumps talking about television and shoes. They weren't quite unfriendly to me, but they were not interested in me either, and so I wallflowered around, keeping myself out of conversations I didn't want to be in, even as I yearned to be invited to participate. So this was high school, I thought: being bored, being lonely.

I stood outside on the front porch. It was a warm night, early enough in the school year that it was still light out, and I debated walking home. But then a few older students from other schools came laughing out onto the porch and said wasn't it a boring party. I said it sure was, and I was relieved—here were people with authority, and they were bored, too. They asked if I wanted to go to a better party, and for the next few months I was with—I wish there was a less silly term for it—a bad crowd. Within minutes I was in a car a teenager was driving, something that had never happened before. Hours later I was kissing someone I didn't know, and then someone else, of another gender. The next weekend I was drunk, and dancing at a club that wasn't supposed to let me in, where I'd some weeks later buy drugs in the parking lot. There were bars, too, that would serve me—gay bars, for the most part. I had some half-formed notion that in these bars, perhaps because it was so dark inside, I looked twenty-one. This of course was not the case. When I think of that time, I wonder why none of the adults in that place told me to go home. Instead one of them said I was sexy, which was the first time anyone had said such a thing to me.

It was a few thrilling, sordid months. These nights felt oceans away from the usual family and homework and the rest of a very ordinary life. But things quickly got boring. The crowd didn't have much to say to each other, really, so we kept our mouths busy with oral sex and horrendous mixtures of alcohol. I should have been terrified, of AIDS most of all, which was snarling its way through the very bars that found me sexy, and sometimes I was. But I was young, and more scared of being busted by my parents, and the terror was the least boring thing about all of it. I was more often sick, or just disgusting. This time has left a lifelong legacy of my overtipping cabdrivers. Back then, cabs being unaffordable, the scam was to give the driver an address close enough to home, and then bolt out the back door at a nearby red light. Once I pulled this scam after vomiting out of the cab window, all down the yellow door. "Thank you," the cabdrivers say now, as I force 80 percent into their hands; "No," I reply, "thank *you*."

Hiding in the bushes, while a driver swore and looked in vain for my shivering self, I realized it was time to stop. One night I failed to meet where we were supposed to meet, and this being before electronic communication, it was easy to slip entirely out of their influence. I found friends my own age, much less wild and much better people. My main drug became caffeine—this was before espresso culture had been installed everyplace, so a place to sit and drink a latte had a distinct and glamorous feel in America, like a subtitled film or a perfume ad in a magazine. On weekends a handful of us would have a few rounds at one café, then troop over to another for more. We talked about what all teenagers talk about: nothing. We did it a lot. Jittery from five or six shots of espresso, flush with conversation instead of sex, I liked how being bored brought me to a new kind of shivery boredom. From Baudelaire, I learned the word *ennui* for this beautiful space, a time in my life when I was all possibility and no execution.

We were a tight group, but a loose affiliation, drifting alternately away from and too close to one another, the way one does. At any given moment there were about eight of us hanging out. *The Basic Eight* became the title of my first novel, which contains a melodramatic and murderous plot but still manages mostly to be about a group of high school students hanging out. (My wife's Florida grandmother read it and summed it up as "Talk, talk, talk.") We liked an elegant setting or activity—an outdoor sculpture garden to dance in after hours, someone's parent-free house for a multicourse dinner party, a bar called The White Room With the Blue Glow, which served only water. There was a big hotel downtown, with a glitzy bar on the top floor for which we had neither the funds nor the birthdates. Instead, we'd get in the elevator and press the button for the floor just below, then walk down the hallway to a fire exit which, contrary to signage, did not sound alarm when opened. There was a fire escape where you could sit and do nothing and look out at the city and sky. My vertigo made me too afraid to go out there, but also afraid to say so, so I stood in the doorway of the emergency exit, watching my friends watching the city. Boredom could inspire things but ghastly and glamorous. I watched my friends, lounging on the rusty metal, and thought of a lyric by the deadpan pop duo Pet Shop Boys:

> We've lost all our money, we're thrown out of bars,
> We're lying in the gutter but we're looking at the stars.

although it would be a few years before I knew they'd nicked that from Oscar Wilde.

Eventually we got caught, of course. Some paying guest ratted us out, and hotel security escorted us back down to the lobby and took our names. My friend Matt, whom I called "Mattathias" in imitation of Orson Welles calling Joseph Cotten "Jedediah" in *Citizen Kane*, told the guy "Stanley Kubrick," carefully spelling it out for him. I said I was Jim Jarmusch, then and now my favorite filmmaker. His style is most often described as "deadpan," although detractors tend to use the word "boring," which I think is actually the more accurate and admirable description. His films have the pace of hanging out and spacing out. Obvious cues for significance—music, visible emotion— are absent or so off base as to be bootless. Jarmusch has brought this perspective and practice to a variety of genres—a Western, a vampire movie, a romantic comedy, a martial arts flick, a spy caper—but back when I was in high school, he only had three movies to his name, including *Permanent Vacation*, a movie that was not released theatrically and thus completely unavailable to me, a situation perfect for cult fandom in adolescence.

Stranger than Paradise was the one I really liked, and one scene in particular kept playing in my head. Our heroes decide to go see Lake Erie in the dead of winter, driving through a desolate landscape, blindingly white with snow, something even more blank and striking when filmed in the grainy black and white. They get out, very cold, and walk to a metal railing at the edge of the lake, where they stand and look at another vast, white expanse of nothing, almost identical to where they've trooped over from. "Beautiful," one of them says, after, and before, a long staring pause—a joke, I guess, but there's something about the pace, the setup, that makes it something else. It is not beautiful, this nothing view of the lake, but somehow staring at it, boring as it is, makes me believe it might be so. I found this something refreshingly different from so many literal and manipulative tropes in mainstream film, that boredom, something we were always told was bad, was the whole point. The empty, snowy landscape was like a blank sheet of paper, the world's most inspiring thing, from which could come something wonderful.

This principle, a faith in a certain boring vacancy at the heart of artistic endeavor, has kept me company a long time. I went to college in a miserable little town, for instance, its meager bragging rights that it was more or less equidistant from Boston and New York City—three hours, by bus. The bus line was called Peter Pan, and each bus was named after something in the *Peter Pan* pantheon, a sad literary legacy if there ever was one. There must have been early buses named Captain Hook or Wendy, but those were long rusted away, and by the time I was riding Peter Pan, the buses were called things like Come Away, Come Away and the Old Tree Stump. Climbing aboard the Old Tree Stump on a Friday was lonely business. The passengers were the usual mix, and I'm sure all of them—well, some—had rich and full lives brimming with laughter and joy. But we were all alone on the bus. Outside, highways were ugly Jarmusch landscapes, and when it got dark and I'd miss seeing even the ugliness, instead of the pitch black rectangle of the window. The dreariness of the Old Tree Stump meant that I stayed lonely the whole time.

I always brought a book, of course. Not quite by design and not quite by coincidence—by instinct, I guess—I read books in which loneliness is ennobled and important—Amos Oz's *Black Box*, in which a mass of desperate, misread correspondence only pushes a family further apart from one another, or Haruki Murakami's *A Wild Sheep Chase*, in which a man with nothing much to do stumbles into a vast and mysterious conspiracy. (Public transportation is still one of my favorite places to read—I once let my usual bus take me to the end of the line, just so I could finish Nafkote Tamirat's *The Parking Lot Attendant*.) It is often said that literature makes one less lonely, and I suppose the case can be made that Professor Gideon and his family, or the mysterious Sheep Man, were keeping me company on these long bus rides. Reading wasn't a cure for loneliness but framed it as part of a long tradition of people feeling alienated and isolated all over this teeming planet.

I was now sufficiently lonely, I thought, to start writing fiction, and I dutifully applied for a slot in the fiction writing class taught by the Famous Author. This required an interview, so I put on a nice shirt and went to her office to present my meager credentials—some poems published in high school journals. I say "meager" because that's the word she used for them, something that seemed mean at the time and unconscionable now. (I was nineteen. What sort of credentials was she expecting?) She told me that for the first class session, we would each be assigned a poem of her own choosing for us to memorize, and that we would meet in a field full of leaves—I remember that phrase, *field full of leaves*, which somehow makes both the field and the leaves seem ugly—to recite them. I left her office feeling like a first-year medical student fainting at the sight of blood. I did not like her, I didn't like the poem she chose, and I did not want to stand in a field full of leaves reciting things. Maybe I didn't want to be a writer after all.

A few days later I was invited to some sort of student dinner, and found myself seated next to another writer and teacher I'd never heard of. She told me two things I found interesting: that the title of her first novel was *Mother Isn't Dead, She's Only Sleeping*, and that in *her* fiction writing class, each student turned in ten pages a week and met with her, individually, in her kitchen, to talk about them. This was my mentor, Kit Reed. I signed right up.

Kit Reed's work sprawls uncategorizably across various genres and boundaries. Science fiction is the most frequent pigeonhole, but I'm always startled when I spot her name in an old sci-fi journal, one of the few women alongside the likes of Isaac Asimov and Philip K. Dick. Nor does it feel right to see her in various all-female groupings, whether in a fantastical mode, with the likes of Marion Zimmer Bradley and Octavia Butler, or in a realistic mode—"domestic," it's often queasily labelled— with Lois Gould or Alison Lurie. The best I can describe her work is that it's about mostly normal people coping with something strange happening, related in prose that is accessible and concise and yet off-kilter in a way that's tricky to unfurl. Of course, that's basically a description of all the best literature.

What it meant to study fiction writing with someone whose work evades easy categorization is that she had no patience for the pretensions of writing. The hierarchies of genre, the strict expectations of style, the boxes and lanes in which you're supposed to sit or stay held no water with Kit Reed. She was interested in helping you figure out what it was you might be trying to do, and helping you find strategies by which you might achieve your desired effect. This was in stark relief to so many writing classes, in which some favorite writer of the instructor is held up as a perfect example of something or other—William Trevor, for example, all well and good if you want to write in the same brilliant way William Trevor does. If you're looking for a different kind of brilliance, however, you need something else.

Kit worked with people who were writing prose poems about queer desire and people working on pulpy novels about werewolves, people who wanted to be Virginia Woolf and people who wanted to be Aaron Spelling. The strategies she recommended were individually tailored, but they all had the same method: go read something. "I think if you read more Isak Dinesen you might figure out the ending to your story," she'd say, or "You need to figure out when to write dialog and when to keep with description. How much James Baldwin have you read?" Her suggestions had that polite phrasing, "more" or "how much," as if you were a well-read peer. As with turning in ten pages a week, quantity was a big part of the game. A beginning writer has lots and lots of bad prose to write, and as much good prose to read, so the idea was to get started and keep going. "You're trying a Muriel Spark thing," Kit told me once, correctly. "Read some more Muriel Spark novels."

I had not heard of Muriel Spark. "How many?" I asked, and she looked at me with the irritation I feel on my face sometimes nowadays, toward young people with no responsibilities and tons of time on their hands.

"They're short," she said. "Read a bunch."

Read a bunch sounded casual and sloppy, but as with Kit's

shortcake recipe—"It's a drump (about 1/2 a big kitchen scoop) of shortening and a bunch of flour and baking powder prolly a half teaspoon and probably a quarter to a third a cup of sugar and muckle it up and add milk until it looks okay"—it added up to something delicious. Kit's own bracing sentences have that enviable quality of feeling knocked together, but exhibit a careful, powerful breadth when you stare hard at them. One of her stories starts up

> In the mountains tonight, in the jagged hills below the observatory, the Girl Scouts' voices ring out—just not where you can hear, for the missing girls of Troop 13 are as wary as they are spirited.

and look how that opening description disorients you a little—"mountains" takes us up, "below the observatory," takes us down, so the startle of "just not where you can hear" strikes us even harder. "Wary" and "spirited" lay out the tone—there's something eerie about "missing girls," and something comic about the fact that they're Girl Scouts.

The shortcake would bake (greased cookie sheet, 350, 30 minutes-ish), and we'd sit at her kitchen table and go over a lousy paragraph of mine one more time. "You're telling me everything in a row here," she'd say. "What did you say about that Muriel Spark you liked?"

"*Not to Disturb?* That it felt like a mystery."

"And in a mystery . . . ?" she prompted, patiently.

"We find out things gradually," I said, and four drafts later I had something sort of OK.

The shortcake was dessert. I'd signed up for the latest time slot, which meant that sometimes I was invited to dinner. There might be another guest—a visiting poet with stories of academic backstabbing, a former student with a rough cut of his vampire movie—but often it was just me and Kit and her husband, Joe Reed, a fabled figure on campus. He wore a cowboy hat and boots, and drank iced tea from large, wide-mouthed containers meant to hold other things. I'd walked by his office door, which was decorated with a quote from a student review laid out in plastic letters: "Reed's not as pompous as he's cracked up to be." When Joe clunked into the kitchen, he didn't seem pompous, just loud, especially when he laughed. He laughed a lot. We all did.

Joe taught in the American Studies department, his classes often divided into units on American individuals, and the juxtapositions would be jarring first, then illuminating: John Philip Sousa and John Wayne, Malcolm X and Adrienne Rich, Busby Berkeley and Albert Ayler. He was interested in how things bumped up together, how the sublimated rage in the music of Scott Joplin, concealed in his jaunty melodies, could be found in the prose of William Faulkner, say, or how the busy gaze of Walt Whitman helped give birth to the brassy corn of Cecile B. DeMille. His lectures were in the afternoon, and at night, once a week, he'd introduce a movie. Movies were his favorite thing. As with Kit and literature, he found meaning and delight in any kind of movie. Not *all* movies—he was loud and scathing when he found something unforgivable—but old epics and recent blockbusters, serious independent efforts and quick genre pieces, things nobody watched and things everyone's seen.

(An old classmate of mine maintains that the happiest moment in his life is when Joe Reed said one evening, after weeks of watching old silents, "Tonight's movie is *Aliens*.") The Reeds laid out for me an astonishing variety of approaches, to making art and to getting through life, centered around the idea that none of this knowledge was hierarchical, that there was no better way, only a way you preferred—that everyone, in other words, was making it up as they went along, standing in their own circles by themselves.

After dinner I usually left to return to a normal college life of post-structuralist argument and *De La Soul Is Dead*, but sometimes I'd hang around while they watched something—*Twin Peaks*, *She's Gotta Have It*, *Moon Over Miami*, *They Were Expendable*, you never knew what—and Joe would stretch out on an old psychiatrist's couch with an easel tilted over it, so he could paint while he watched. He painted like Kit wrote—something strange was always happening: the First Ladies of the United States frolicking on the moon, a bunch of ants reenacting the Boston Massacre, Chairman Mao enjoying a day at the beach. He was going through a phrase where he painted a lot of alphabets dedicated to some theme or historical figure. I have one on my wall—<u>A</u>lice B. Toklas, <u>B</u>rothers of hers, her old easy <u>C</u>hair, etc.—dedicated to Gertrude Stein.

Joe told me to read Stein, and because he was right about *Venom*, an early '80s movie in which an accidental mamba mix-up (yes) complicates Klaus Kinski's kidnapping plot, I figured he'd be right about this, too. I had a very vague picture of Gertrude Stein in my head—she was the lesbian pal of Picasso and Hemingway, right?—but I hadn't read any of her books. But in another way I had been looking for her for a few years, since encountering a parody of her work.

A side effect of our relentlessly self-amused culture is that people, especially young people, can encounter a satirical version of something before they've met the genuine article, if they ever do. There's something so powerful, so prominent, about some cultural tropes that they ring true even when they're being rung sarcastically. We see Bugs Bunny or Homer Simpson saunter through the swinging saloon doors long before we encounter a bona fide Western; most children's first vampire is the Count on *Sesame Street*, a parody of Bela Lugosi, whose actual work they may never see. More than a few children have brought me a copy of *The Flowers of Evil*, wondering if Charles Baudelaire's name is a sly wink at the Baudelaire orphans of *A Series of Unfortunate Events*, instead of vice versa. In this case, it was something I came across in high school, when I was plodding my way through *The Fountainhead*. There are few writers I have enjoyed less than Ayn Rand, who combines didactic philosophy and hysterical melodrama in a way that spoils any fun you might find in either. Nevertheless, one little section struck me:

> " . . . toothbrush in the jaw toothbrush brush brush tooth jaw foam dome in the foam Roman dome come home home in the jaw Rome dome tooth toothbrush toothpick pickpocket socket rocket . . ."
>
> Peter Keating squinted his eyes, his glance unfocused as for a great distance, but put the book down. The book was thin and black, with scarlet letters forming: *Clouds*

and Shrouds by Lois Cook. The jacket said that it was a record of Miss Cook's travels around the world.

This is a parody—a pretty weak and mean one—of Gertrude Stein, but I didn't know that. I knew I wasn't supposed to like it—Peter Keating is an object of ridicule in the novel, for, among other weaknesses, listening to other people—and I knew it wasn't real. But I wanted it. I *liked* those toothbrushes knocking around and I wanted to read *Clouds and Shrouds.*

The campus bookstore had the next best thing, a copy of Stein's *The Making of Americans,* which I decided to read one boring, lonely summer. I rented an apartment in Boston with my girlfriend and a couple of other pals, who were all working and taking classes. My seizures and hallucinations were in high dudgeon, which made me unemployable, even by the generous standards of undergraduates on break. I spent my time trying to get better. It didn't work. I had some doctors and some drugs—I remember buying, and being fascinated by, one of those guillotines for halving your dosage of pills—but I did not improve. Furthermore, the weather was horrid—sweaty and blazing. The apartment had a vinyl recliner someone had left behind, and I would sit reading in my underwear, unsticking myself when I got up to pour myself more cold water. This couldn't last, and it didn't. I put my pants on and went outside.

I would walk until I found someplace where I could sit and read—someplace air-conditioned, hopefully—and then I'd order an iced coffee and read until I felt, from the New England passive-aggressiveness in the place, that I'd stayed too long, or until a seizure hit and I assured the staff I was all right. Then

I'd walk to another place and do the same thing. I buzzed all day in thrall to the way each of the worlds I was in—the flow of words on the page, the clatter of the streets around me, the manic electricity of my own troubled brain—bumped up against one another. I was the only one, the only one in the world, to feel this crazed intersection.

Loneliness has a sad reputation. But all it is is a small circle you are standing in. This might be a sad experience, if it is not where you want to be standing. But being lonely often has the magic of clear truth—a reminder that the circle is always present, in your mind, and that you alone can invite others to join you, the way you alone can decide what book to read, what sentences to hold close or to skip entirely. The pleasure of reading is the pleasure of loneliness. Loneliness is at the heart of literature—every book, every single book you can read. This shouldn't be surprising, as literature is just a byproduct of writing—alone and frowning, as I am now, over a piece of paper, to try and get something down correctly—and writing is in turn a byproduct of private thoughts.

I spent that whole lonely summer on Gertrude Stein's endless, and endlessly difficult, *The Making of Americans*, which begins deceptively:

> Once an angry man dragged his father along the ground through his own orchard. "Stop!" cried the groaning old man at last. "Stop! I did not drag my father beyond this tree."

I liked this a lot, although it turned out to be wholly unrepresentative of the book and author both. Most of Stein's writing, and the vast majority of the nine-hundred-plus pages of *The Making of Americans*, is much more difficult to read. A more typical passage goes like this:

> All three of them then began to have in them their own individual feeling, there was beginning soon in each one of them the being alone inside, each one of them in their own feeling. They were different each one of them from the others of them in the troubles they had then inside them, in the lonely feeling they had sometimes in them that they were alone each one in them, in the scared feeling they could have in them, in the hurt or angry feelings each one in their own way had inside them.

Stein's sentences chew things over, some idea or memory or just some sonorous phrase, in little stop-starts and double-backs that aren't quite sentences and don't need to be. You can't lay out writing like this, word by word, in your mind; it's like picking up rice from the floor grain by grain. It's better for things to get swept away. No one remembers the plot, if one can be discerned, of a Gertrude Stein book, and despite her conspicuous enthusiasm for playing with language, there is little of her prose that sticks precisely in the mind. (Indeed, her oft-quoted, "A rose is a rose is a rose," is inaccurate. The first word is "Rose," the name of the book's main character.) I can't say that reading Stein's sentences as I wandered around the sweltering streets of Boston was an unmitigated delight. I might have stopped reading it, had I anything else to do.

The Making of Americans hit me in a new way—less precisely, perhaps, than the exquisite clarity of so many other writers, but more resonantly, as if the muddle of the text left me more room to think about it, a perfect space, in a fiercely noisy mind, to dwell in gorgeous ennui. The summer ended, and my girlfriend stayed in Boston, the better for us to break up several more times. My friends broke up, too, and drifted away from me into their own crises, but *The Making of Americans* stayed with me. Back on campus for my last year of college, I reported triumphantly to Joe that I'd read Stein's masterwork; he laughed, loudly, and said, "Oh, I never managed to get through that," and there I was, as lonely as ever.

Then it was time to get a job. I'd been privileged enough in my life thus far that I'd had some employment here and there, but as a sort of novelty for pocket money and to give me a window into experience. After graduating it was time to get a real job—you know, where everyone hates you and you know nothing, and which is, despite all this drama, very boring. Mine was being an administrative assistant at the Computer Science Department at the City College of San Francisco. It was a part-time job but paid enough for me to live with my new love in a little apartment and spend my afternoons trying to capture the feeling of adolescent ennui in my meandering first draft of *The Basic Eight*, as long as we didn't buy anything besides used paperbacks and cans of black beans. I commuted to this job on a streetcar, which is even more lonely than a bus, because a streetcar is pretending to be a train, sitting there on tracks as if it's about to race off someplace. Everyone loves trains—all those things whizzing by the window make you feel glamorous and busy—and so a streetcar is like vegetarian meat, sadly pretending that you will sadly pretend it is a slice of chicken. I read the cheapest books I could find—big thick paperbacks, editions of another type of literature in which loneliness is paramount: gothic literature. I read a Horace Walpole omnibus featuring *The Castle of Otranto*, in which the hapless heroine loses her husband in a helmet accident—you read that right—and then, fleeing the sinister and lecherous contrivances of various factions of in-laws, ends up in a cave just dark enough for mistaken identity, and I read Ann Radcliffe's *The Mysteries of Udolpho*, thick as a hoagie, in which the hapless heroine loses her parents and, feeling the sinister if not quite lecherous contrivances of her aunt, ends up in a castle just dark enough for assorted hauntings.

This was all perfect for a lonely streetcar ride. I had sent the working draft of *The Basic Eight*, more than four hundred pages long, to poor Charlotte Sheedy, and I began to toy with an idea for a new book: a mock-gothic novel, ambiguously anachronistic, about a lonely young man who is married off to an evil countess—or maybe a count, I liked the idea of queering it up—and moves into a remote and creaky castle full of sinister goings-on. The working title was *A Series of Unfortunate Events*, and, perhaps appropriately, it wasn't going very well. The snag was keeping my protagonist helpless. So many Gothic novels rest on the principle that a terrified young woman—wandering the moors, or closely watched on a family estate—has nowhere else to go, what with various conniving patriarchal forces. My hero, meanwhile, could just call a cab and get out of there. It took me another five years or so to realize that if the hero were a child—or a set of siblings, perhaps, so they could talk to one another, providing dialog—*A Series of Unfortunate Events* would go much better. For now I just brooded about it, when I was supposed to be working.

My new girlfriend had a job, also boring and lonely, so our little household had creative energy to burn. She took design and illustration classes, drawing up plans for CD box sets and museum signage that existed only in assignments; I played accordion in a band, Tzamboni, which offered its shambling, ill-rehearsed brand of "fake world music" in bars to small groups of indulgent friends. And together we started a zine called *American Chickens!*, a tiny publication printed on one side of an ordinary sheet of paper and then folded repeatedly so it was about the size of a matchbox. We distributed our zine by leaving small stacks in unnoticed corners and shelves in cafés, bars and the occasional bank lobby. The zine was produced—that is, we made copies of it—at Kinko's, one of a chain of copy places, now mostly swallowed up, that was a bustling center of people making their own fun. There were fleets of copy machines, with little tables alongside strewn with tape and scissors and other people's projects in progress: visual art, promotional flyers, wedding albums, party invitations, an array of freedom of expression, all amateur and all on paper. It felt like home.

Around this time, small publications of a somewhat different sort were arriving at my job—tiny neighborhood newspapers, with names like the *Parkside Express* and the *Nob Hill Gazette*, which for some reason were delivered to the Computer Science Department at the City College of San Francisco. I knew better than to ask my boss what to do with them. His office door was shut all day long, and my central duty had become shooing away, in person and on the phone, anyone who tried to see him.

I knew what the trouble was, but nobody said it out loud, even him. He'd put on my desk a little piece of paper he'd brought to a meeting, instead of saying it out loud to his boss. *I have AIDS*, it said. I did what I could for him, which wasn't much. In sending students and faculty to other people's offices, I hope I managed to give him some privacy.

Working for a dying man slowed things down at the office, and I began to read each of these tiny, harmless newspapers cover to cover in order to find the tiniest, most harmless article in them. Then I would compose, on the typewriter of the Computer Science Department at the City College of San Francisco—because that's what I had on my desk, at the Computer Science Department, a typewriter—outraged letters to the editor regarding these articles. If an official announced that street-cleaning schedules had changed, I would point out that the shift from Tuesdays to Fridays was probably rooted in anti-Semitism. If they were giving away balloons at a park, I would accuse them of trying to choke birds with the popped rubber remnants. Anti-litter editorials were obviously insensitive to avant-garde sculpture, you know, things like that.

The letters all had two things in common: they all began with the sentence "How dare you!," a phrase I liked for its unconvincing hysteria and obscure grammatical construction, and they closed not with my own name, but a name I had devised while on the phone with a right-wing political group. In the name of researching *The Basic Eight*, in which the heroine's murder becomes the subject of much right-wing-media hullaballoo, I'd spent time calling conservative organizations I found ridiculous and asking them to mail me their materials, the better to mock

them in my novel in progress. During one such call, the conservative woman on the phone asked me for my name and for
some reason I panicked. *Don't give your name to these people*, I
thought, and so I instead sputtered the first thing that came into
my head: *Lemony Snicket.*

There was a pause, blank and empty, during which I marveled
at my own idiocy. Who could possibly be dimwitted enough to
believe that was anyone's real name? And then the conservative
woman said to me, "Is that spelled how it sounds?" and I said
yes, and asked her to read it back to me, because I had no idea
how it sounded.

When pamphlets began appearing at our apartment with
this name on it, I was stuck with it. It became the name we gave
to homemade cocktails and desserts, a name we gave at coffee-
houses and pizza places, just to hear some poor guy say, "Large
mushroom and artichoke for..." One birthday, Mattathias
gave me a set of Lemony Snicket business cards, which I began
giving out at bars. Besides my address and phone number, the
card said "Rhetorical Analysis," which took a number of forms
when I was forced to explain myself to strangers. Sometimes I
said I was a yacht lawyer, a phrase I had overheard someplace,
which meant, I explained, that I represented the interests of
the yacht, rather than any of the sailors or other seafolk. The
off-center digressions, the unreliable philosophy, the belief in
literature as a desperate cure for ennui—all of the hallmarks of
Lemony Snicket were right there, alongside my stumbly gothic
novel. It became part of a regular routine for my household: dull
office jobs in the morning, attempts at art-making in the afternoon, weekend nights in taquerias, followed by nightcap net-

working for Mr. Snicket, bleary the next morning with poached eggs and indie rock.

One of my favorite indie albums was *Wasps' Nests* by the 6ths, one of a few bands helmed by Stephin Merritt. I'd picked up the album after reading somewhere that both the name of the band and the title of the album had been chosen because they're very difficult to say on the radio. This was enough for me to like them, and when I played the album I was additionally entranced.

The first song, "San Diego Zoo," has an elegant little melody—instantly catchy, the notes rising and falling in a pattern that seems both striking and inevitable. The instrumentation sounds like toys, and the voice sounds bored, but there's an ache underneath. Similarly, the chorus starts out describing a road trip in ordinary language and landmarks—

> Highway 405 will take you
> From the Boom Boom Room
> To Interstate 5 which goes right to
> The San Diego Zoo

—that might seem the very definition of boredom. But then, in the last line—

> How could I have ever left you?

we see that the banal route is a heartbroken retracing of steps—that something's gotten away despite it all being mapped out. It's a sad song, made all the sadder by Mr. Merritt's understated, slightly clunky execution. It's not boredom; it's ennui.

I say "Mr. Merritt" because that's what I call him. We've now worked together for more than twenty years and largely prefer to address each other with a distant formality that provides a nice space in which to work. We met when my girlfriend and I moved the *American Chickens!* headquarters to Manhattan—that is, when she got into grad school and I tagged along. The boyfriend of a friend of the sister of an old roommate of mine mentioned that someone he knew had interviewed this songwriter I'd mentioned admiring. From this dubious connection I learned that Mr. Merritt wrote songs every afternoon in an Irish diner in the East Village with the worst bread in Christendom. When I arrived, Mr. Merritt was halfway through his second or third pot of black tea, writing in a notebook. I introduced myself and mentioned the Henry James novel *The Spoils of Poynton*, in which three people argue about furniture, as a possible source for a stage musical. We became friends. In his notebook was his idea for his main band, the Magnetic Fields, a stage show with three-record set to match, called *69 Love Songs*, and so there was a lot of work to be done. I tagged along when I could, playing a few instruments here and there, but mostly just watching him work. He recorded the album almost entirely himself and almost entirely in his tiny studio apartment, with keyboards stacked up on racks, guitars and other stringed things strung up everywhere, and milk crates full of bonkers percussion, imported harmonicas, and noisy toys. The sessions were largely a matter of filling in the blanks. An arrangement might begin with some instrument Mr. Merritt hadn't used in a while, and then would continue with whatever seemed missing—a bassline on some broken thing, a countermelody on something re- or de-tuned, maracas as drumsticks and tambourines as drums, microphones too far or too close. Mr. Merritt is often accused of being a perfectionist, but he's a bit of the opposite, a devout corraller of happy accidents, encouraging musicians to try the wrong approach, the bonkers note, anything to fill in the blanks.

Those were long days in Mr. Merritt's apartment working on the album, and finishing the record was only the beginning of the story, as *69 Love Songs* was released and I kept tagging along with its growing reception and influence. I shared larger and larger stages with the Magnetic Fields, playing *69 Love Songs* and the albums that followed, watching him write, record and generally make magic from boredom. But the day I always remember with him was not magic; it was bad. He and I were at the diner, hopped up on black tea and trying to work on the Henry James musical, which had become science fiction. Nothing worked. Our ideas went from worse to bad and back again. By the end of the day, we were both so cranky that it might have seemed like disagreement, though we were in perfect accord that both of us were morons without one good scheme between us. We lapsed into silence and split the bill, agreeing to meet the next day and deciding where and how we might start up again. I walked him to his favorite bar, a mortifying place called Dick's with a throbbing sign to match.

"This was a good day," he said, when we reached the door.

"What the hell are you talking about?" or something, I sputtered. "We didn't do anything."

He smiled a little, I can see it now, a cold day, dark early, gray all over the place. Mr. Merritt, more characteristically, didn't say anything for a minute, and then he didn't say anything at all. He just let it happen around us, the blank ennui of not getting anything done providing the space to do something better tomorrow, and to feel better right away. It worked. I felt better, and I had something to bring home, for all the frustrating work days I had ahead of me. He smiled, sort of, and went into the bar, one of the artists I admire most in the world, never boring but, almost always, a little bored.

11

Problematic.

I was working in a bookstore in San Francisco when a man, a customer in a suit but no tie, asked me if I was eighteen. I was offended, having turned eighteen literally months before. He clarified his reason for asking, and I spent the summer in secret with him. It wasn't the first time I'd been with a man, but no one knew that I had done such a thing, and no one knew now. He was in his early thirties, a grownup, living the life of a grownup; the secret was easy to keep because I was suddenly in places which hardly overlapped with my actual life. We went to hear chamber music—he was a classical musician, something adults did—in auditoriums I'd never heard of, and ate dinner in restaurants too expensive for anyone I normally spent time with. He paid for everything, not just picking up the bill but pressing money into my hand when I wanted a coffee or a bottle of water. This seemed glamorous, like the older men slipping Holly Golightly money in *Breakfast At Tiffany's*, which I'd just read. The man's parents were dead, and had left him enough money, along with a pair of Victorian flats. He lived in one, another adult space, where we'd do grownup things like drink mulled wine and have sex. I didn't like getting dressed at the end of the night to go back to my parents' house, clearly an immature thing to be doing.

At the end of the summer I was scheduled to leave for college, but the man offered me the other flat, at reduced rent, instead—somewhere to live while I figured stuff out. I'm pretty sure I laughed. I wasn't stupid. I could figure stuff out in college—that's what college was for—and in any case I didn't feel confused. The confusion came when he reacted—offended, angry—and I was at last able to pinpoint what was running under our relationship, or whatever you would call it. It was terror, just a little bit of it. I thought I was just nervous about being found out. His immaturity, which had at first made our summer seem inoffensive, was an unnerving characteristic in a grownup, and I got out of there and never saw him again. I still remember the book I left behind.

Is there a word for what happened? I call it a mistake, just a mistake. It does not feel big enough to be, say, a disaster. Everyone notices a disaster, and this had been a secret, an experience that zipped closed, invisible and tidy, when it was over. If I looked for him, if I found him and asked him, I assume he would say the same thing, shaking his head at his behavior the way I shake my head at mine. He shouldn't have approached me, I guess, and I shouldn't have accepted the offer, although initially the offer was a cup of coffee. Maybe he should have known better, but he didn't, and neither did I. He was a grownup, though, and I wasn't, so I can be forgiven for not really knowing what

I was doing. But in fact I *was* a grownup, technically—that's why he'd asked my age straightaway—and I did know what I was doing; it just isn't what I'd do now, which is what I'd say about many, many things I did when I was eighteen, such as finding Holly Golightly's life glamorous. His actions seem, maybe, a little predatory, but I don't really think I was preyed upon. I dislike the proclivity to label so many reconsidered experiences as harmful, especially if they didn't cause harm. The one harmed in this story, it seems to me, is the young man with dead parents and too much money. But if a thirty-year-old friend asked me if they should romance an eighteen-year-old bookstore clerk, I'd say no, they shouldn't. Why not? Because it's harmful. I think. Isn't it?

This is a literary question. Really, it is. I have never liked when authors say their books are like their children, especially after witnessing childbirth, which is clearly much more difficult than being copyedited. But books are in some ways like other people's children. You rarely get to see them made, and then suddenly they are just gallivanting around and nobody can figure out whose responsibility they are. Looking at them, it's difficult to imagine they could be any real trouble—they're so little, even the big ones—but still sometimes it seems maybe somebody's going to get hurt. I don't believe literature can harm anyone, and I certainly don't think any book causes trauma. But why don't I? If I believe literature can heal, even save people's lives, then it seems suspect to dismiss wholeheartedly any claim that this enormous power might somehow cause distress. Literature is made of words, not sticks and stones, but everyone can remember the words that have hurt them, better than we can describe any stick or stone that's clobbered us. I've read things I've hated, things that made me sick. But what sort of sickness am I talking about? Do I mean they caused a powerful emotional effect, which is exactly what literature is supposed to do? Or do I mean something else?

Name a child, and everyone will give the child things with the child's name on it. Thus, in my childhood bedroom was a copy of *Danny, the Champion of the World*, by Roald Dahl. It will come as no surprise to any reader that Dahl's work has had a tremendous influence on me, and it's easy to spot: a typical Dahl novel (*Charlie and the Chocolate Factory*, say, or *Matilda*) moves through a fantastical but familiar world laced with carefully detailed portrayals and discussion of wickedness, and all this doubtless sounds familiar to Snicket fans. I come by this copycatting honestly, having read and reread Dahl to tatters, and what burned in my brain most ferociously was this oft-overlooked work on my shelf. (The plot concerns the hunting of pheasant, and so the book is often moved out of the reach of children, who presumably might join a pheasant-hunting gang if they read such a thing.) It begins,

> When I was four months old, my mother died suddenly
> and my father was left to look after me all by himself. This
> is how I looked at the time.

—and then there is a photograph of a baby, smack dab on the page. "We lived in an old caravan behind a filling station," the book continues, setting up a lifelong housing dream for a certain slice of readership, and then on page two, "here I am on my fifth birthday," and then there's a drawing, by Jill Bennett in my edition, of a young boy. The photograph and the drawing, the drawing and the photograph; I spent so long with page one and page two and page one again. The photograph felt like something in an album, or maybe a textbook—that is, something which really happened. The drawing was something more familiar from other books—it was made up, to go with the words and make them seem real even when they weren't. I was old enough to know that the narrator and the author were different people, because they had different names—Roald, a name I'd never heard before (and haven't since), and Danny, a name I never used. This book seemed like a fictional story about a real person who lived in a made-up caravan behind a filling station, of which, by the way, there was a photograph on the back of the book, along with the author and his real family. There was a little gap, a thrilling one, between the narrator and the author, between what was true and what couldn't be, a crucial space for a young reader, surrounded everywhere by the usual restrictions, to sit free and think what I liked.

Now, I can see where that led me, twenty years later, writing books about impossible things happening to children, illustrated like fiction, published as truth with a staged photograph of the narrator, rather than the actual author. But back then the only thing it made me think of was stories from the Torah I was hearing in religious school, where we were discouraged from talking about whether or not they were true—not because the question was heresy, as it is in some religions, but because it was beside the point. *If a voice told you to build a boat, what would you do?* is an interesting question. *Could the boat really hold two of every animal?* less so. We sat there in synagogue, talking about imaginary stories as if they might be true, because it led to interesting thoughts.

Here I feel obligated to add that it appears Roald Dahl wasn't fond of people fond of the Torah. His anti-Semitism has been widely reported, so you can look it up yourself, although you may be a bit—*disappointed*, is it?—that it consists of a handful of remarks here and there, in my view grounded less from a philosophy of bigotry than part of Dahl, from all accounts, being a generally rotten person. Lots of authors are rotten—they are like people in that way—and Dahl is likely not the most rotten person anybody can think of, by a long shot. He's not even the rottenest one in this book. Nevertheless, people pop up at regular intervals to say Dahl's books should be avoided, or even removed from the shelf, because of those remarks. Of course, the reason we know about what he said is because he's a widely beloved author. The more visible an artist is, the more such remarks are dredged up and studied, so the reason we know we shouldn't read Roald Dahl is because so many people have read him.

The word in vogue for such cases is *problematic*, a word I've always found funny because it just means someone has a problem with something. It is, of course, a problematic term, because it describes the entire human condition, which is to say it describes nothing. Everybody has a problem with something. We are all like people in that way. The removal of books by people with whom someone has a problem would lead to empty shelves. I don't really need to say this, as it's said whenever an author is deemed problematic who isn't problematic to whomever is saying it. This is in turn met with the idea that we should separate the art from the artist, a tidy and appealing phrase which is of course foolish and impossible. The peculiarities of individual works come from the peculiarities of the individuals who make them. All these peculiarities—*all of them*—are problematic to somebody or other. Luckily, your own choices about preferences, dictating what you decide to read, are problematic, too. You pick up a book and look it over for maybe two seconds and decide it's not your thing. A book makes you cringe, or fills you with delight, but you finish it anyway, or you don't. You want to enjoy something, but an odious thing you've heard about the author spoils your fun, or it doesn't, and you feel sheepish about it, or you don't. Not having a coherent stance on what books you do and don't approve of is, sorry to say, problematic.

The solution, we're then told, is to forgive authors for whatever thing we find problematic, whether on paper or in life. This is the most absurd thing of all, and always makes me think of a conversation I heard when I was in ninth grade, when I was trying out a group of potential friends who were into punk. (Of course I didn't fit in, but maybe you can forgive me for trying.) We were sitting around someplace, listening to loud music I hated, and one of them said, "I'll never forgive the Clash for *Combat Rock*." There was a surly pause, and then another guy replied, "You know, I ran into the Clash the other day, and they were brokenhearted that a random American teenager was never going to forgive them." What he meant, in true ninth grade punk fashion, was *fuck you for thinking the Clash is waiting for your opinion, fuck you for thinking your problematic opinion*— and it is problematic, because even I know that *Cut the Crap* is *way worse*—is what matters about some artwork somebody made. To position your own opinion, even on a bench in high school, as a bona fide attachment to the artist to whom you're responding was a hopelessly stupid and square way of behaving.

This is why you see stupidity and squareness at the heart of dubbing any artist problematic. There is a fantasy at work, that removing some questionable bit of vocabulary, some reference to something objectionable or just some tilt that one might infer means something is being thought about improperly, will result in some sublime something nobody minds at all. Instead, the culture that survives such purges is dull and featureless, often offensively so, the way the music they play in dentists' offices is so unobjectionable as to be infuriating. "The thing is," a wise artist said to me, as he watched his own work battered about in this way, "people with a sense of humor are equally offended by people without a sense of humor as they are by us. We just have a sense of humor about it." The real problematic thing is deciding that the offensive peculiarity of your own taste is something which ought to override the peculiarity of others, rather than realizing there's nothing special about your taste, however fervently it dwells in you.

High school also found me doing a big project on a poet. I chose E. E. Cummings, surely because of the nearby release of the movie *Hannah and Her Sisters*, which I'd seen with my girlfriend and which introduced a generation of bookish romantics to a Cummings poem that's sort of everyone's favorite. You know the one, it ends:

(i do not know what it is about you that closes

and opens; only something in me understands
the voice of your eyes is deeper than all roses)
nobody, not even the rain, has such small hands

a poem you may find liberatingly erotic in its metaphorical frankness, or uncomfortably fetishistic in its objectification, the way a reference to a Woody Allen movie might seem harmless or tasteless. Cummings is that sort of poet, considered both overrated and underrated, ascribed too much profundity in some circles and of none whatsoever in others. This stanza has a sort of wispy efficacy that I found quite seductive, not to mention the poet's casual abuse of punctuation and the fact that my girlfriend really liked it, too. For the project, I was supposed to find out something the poet had said about his own work, which in the pre-internet days was trickier. I remember the encyclopedia in my high school library listed Cummings, who died before I was born, as still alive, and in any case offered nothing more than the sort of biographical sketch that can make any artist sound boring. I walked with my girlfriend to the San Francisco State University Library, where only university students could check out books. But students at my high school had a system, wherein one person would stand in the shrubbery at the side of the building to catch the books their partner in crime would drop out of the second-floor window. I found some academic study of Cummings's work and tossed it into my girlfriend's small hands, but I don't think I cracked it open. Instead I found the poet's own introduction for his collection *is 5*, a loopy, one-page text that contained this little scrap:

It is with roses and locomotives (not to mention acrobats
Spring electricity Coney Island the 4th of July the eyes of
mice and Niagara Falls) that my "poems" are competing.

They are also competing with each other, with elephants, and with El Greco.

Every time I read this I find it bracing—the giddy admission
that the poet finds his own work just crowding together with
all of the other stuff—bits of nature and culture just barging in,
so haphazardly and intrusively that almost as soon as he closes
parentheses full of them, in come elephants and El Greco, along
with the same poems themselves. It shrugs off the deep fantasy
of art: that it is given a rapt, focused audience, and in turn has
a real, traceable effect. This is easily discarded because we knew
it was wrong all along. Nothing makes the mind wander more
than someone telling you they need your undivided attention.
Even in your most fiercely focused hours of reading, when you
lose complete track of your immediate surroundings, when your
coffee gets cold while you finish the chapter, you are still not
alone with the book, because everything in your mind, every
memory each word prompts, every pressing concern, even as the
book turns your eyes in a different direction, clouds the sun of
your attention. You might lose track of time, but time does not
lose track of you. Your life continues, with all of its trappings
and wanderings competing with everything else, and as far as
how the book affects you, it is no more traceable than a grain of
salt in soup. The effect is real, but there's no mapping it, because
the map is not the territory and the territory is the changing
landscape of your mind and the changing world it observes and

inhabits. I have a basement filled with boxes filled with letters from children filled with questions, and the one they ask most is, *is it real?* I know the answer isn't, "No, the *real* thing is a man sitting at a table with a legal pad." My work has not led them astray, even if they are confused; it has not harmed them, even if they are upset. The landscape is too enormous for anything as stupid and square as that. The story is real, even if it's not true—they are living in the space it provides, thinking about what they like, not what people hope they are thinking. This is how literature works, freely offering itself, or failing to, every which way along with everything else in the world. Just this paragraph alone is competing with everything I thought I would write about here, and didn't—a story about Odetta, a mistake in my favorite Virginia Woolf novel, a poem by a white South African about guilt and reading, what a jazz musician said about a long-ago funeral he watched online—not to mention everything already crowding in your brain, elephants and El Greco.

So let me say to you now, if you can hear me over all that, what I think about the curtailing of literature, and I'll say it like the punk I'll never be. Fuck what the author says, and fuck whatever terrible thing may be found in their words. Fuck removing the book from view, and fuck snatching it from someone else's hands. Fuck separating the art from the artist, and fuck forgiving any author for anything. All these actions, the motivations behind them, are not just improper about literature, but predatory toward it. A book moves in the world. It may meet you, in a bookstore, say, and ask you if you want an adventure. Perhaps this sounds interesting to you, perhaps not, perhaps you are unsure. The decision is yours—no one is forcing you to read anything—and you won't really know why you made the decision anyway. As far as consequences, if you even know them, to try measuring and tracing such effects is a foolish enterprise, a square and stupid attempt to bridge an impossible gap, like the one between being young and being old, impossible not because the gap is too enormous but because nobody really knows what it is. You may love the book; it may thrill you or make you sick, right in a row or even simultaneously. Books are like people in this way. And if you find yourself feeling that the book is problematic, all that means is that you have a problem with it, and that's easily solved. Leave the book behind, put your clothes back on, and go home.

12

Everything I write is dumb.

Everything I write is dumb. I sit someplace frowning—like the café I'm in now—and then I write something down on my legal pad and there it is, dumb and alone, or maybe that's me. I poke at it and try to make it, what's the word I'm looking for, *not dumb*. It improves, usually—it would almost have to improve—but the real wrong syntax, the words I've conscripted (*conscripted?*), the apparent ideas I'm apparently thinking I convey, just sit there, utterly disconnected from anything.

It's always been this way. When I was young, people knew I wanted to be a writer—probably because I kept telling them—and often foisted notebooks upon me, as gifts. For a day or so, the fantasy of inscribing wisdom onto various lavishly bound pages was quite entrancing. But everything I wrote was dumb. I knew I was supposed to fill the pages with great wisdom, drafting whole stories and poems, or personal revelations of breathtaking import. But I couldn't hack it. Things popped into my head and I wrote them down, fragmentarily, with no resemblance to what someone had taught me, or I'd made up myself, was the proper writing of proper literature. And then, ashamed of myself, I'd stop. My bedroom held quite the collection of fancy notebooks with writing only on the first few pages.

One of these meager entries, for instance, is something I noticed when I was taken to a local theater troupe's matinee performance of *Murder on the Nile*, by Agatha Christie. I remember the performance pretty well because I was going through a fascination with ancient Egypt, and was disappointed that the play had no Egyptian characters in it—just an assortment of traveling Brits, each with a shadowy secret and/or sinister motive. The only locals are some extremely minor figures—the Steward of the cruising boat on which the play takes place, and some Beadsellers, children who pester the Brits when they arrive.

The first act ended with a cliffhanging burst of gunfire, and as an intermission diversion, the audience was given scraps of paper in which we were to guess the identity of victim and murderer both. After the play was over, the results of the poll were taped up in the lobby, and here is what struck me most, what I wrote down in a notebook: someone had guessed that the Steward would be murdered by the Beadsellers. That's what I wrote down when I got home, in a too-fancy notebook, one of those leathery tomes tied shut with a thick cord like a mortifying book of nerdy spells: *The Steward was murdered by the Beadsellers.* It was such a bright flight of fancy, a cheap joke but also an inventive counternarrative to the stock plot I'd just observed. I loved thinking about it and I still do: in the dead of night, three or four Beadsellers sneaking into the Steward's quarters for a deadly deed, a plot completely overlooked by the repressed and scheming passengers trading barbed bon mots over gin in the salon. But of course I never wrote this story down, or even attached anything else to this stray idea someone had scrawled during intermission. It was just a shred I kept—one I keep on keeping—something that seemed less like being a writer and more like having a bad habit.

My bedroom was an unsurprising mess of such scraps, with shelves full of baskets full of little objects from God knows everywhere, toys and prizes and gifts and souvenirs of every description, all of which had attracted my interest for some brief period of time and then never again until someone suggested I throw one of them away, when each became the dearest thing in the world to me. I had, for instance, thumbtacked over a closet door, a scrap of paper I'd ripped away from some packaging that surrounded my father's dry-cleaning, which read, *Here's your freshly ironed shirt, sir! Be sure and have a pleasant day!* Something about it—the wording, the font, just the fact that it sat there on my wall—brought me great joy in the mornings, when I took a quick look in the mirror as I changed into clothes never ever freshly ironed. (Meanwhile, my mother had a scrap of paper taped to her mirror for many years, which she'd taken off a souvenir from Monticello, a facsimile copy of the Declaration of Independence. It read, *Looks Old and Feels Old!*) I don't think about that dry cleaning paper very often, but now that I am thinking about it, I would do anything to have it in my hands.

Back then I would hold rocks in my hands sometimes, while I read or stared out the window. They were rocks I'd picked up on beaches or just walking around. I liked how they felt in my hands, specific with shape but shaped like nothing but themselves. But I knew this was dumb. Every child was supposed to be interested in something of which there were many examples that needed to be acquired. For a brief period of time, it was decided somehow that I collected rocks, and we set up a little table in the corner where I put them. But I didn't want to collect rocks. I tried to read about the different types of rocks—ignominious, cemetery, basilisk—but it made me feel dumb.

> The world can sate the giant appetite
> of children keen on stamps and atlases.
> How vast it all is in the lantern's light!
> How pitiful in recollection's eyes!

This is from "Voyaging," a Baudelaire poem I've had taped up in my brain for most of my life. I never know quite what to make of it. There's something churlish about the opening—casting insults at the meager imaginations of children's hobbies—but there's also something so familiar in the melancholy of those last two lines, the way the world begins to shrink at the first creepings of adolescence. At the age I first encountered this poem, I was experiencing what all of us experience in adolescence: when the place you live turns stifling and dull, and the people who love you transform quickly into enraging, stultifying dorks. Now everything is dumb, not just you, and you can't wait to get out of there.

> One dawn we ship out with our minds aflame
> and hearts surcharged with raw, bitter emotions
> and sail on, with the breakers keeping time,
> rocking our boundlessness in finite oceans.

The labelling of the ocean as "finite" really stuck with me—a locale in *A Series of Unfortunate Events* is called the Finite Forest, an unheeded reminder to the owner of the lumbermill—especially in contrast to our own infinite "boundlessness," an appeal to adolescent self-centeredness if ever there was one. One might even ask why you'd travel the finite ocean at all, if your own self has more exciting breadth. Baudelaire attempts an explanation, a few stanzas later:

> The true voyagers, though, are those who leave
> just to be leaving. Their hearts all buoyancy,
> they, never fading in their fatal drive,
> always say, "Onward!" without knowing why.

Without knowing why. Throughout the poem, Baudelaire delivers his tribute to the great exploratory heroes, all the while layering on a little quiet doubt, identifying their constant restlessness as a pathology as much as it is a spirit of adventure. (It reminds me of a group of aging musicians who gigged together as the Can't Stop Rockin' tour—it sounded not like a commitment to music, but some sort of nervous condition in which they simply could not stop rockin'.) What I think draws me to "Voyaging" is the admission that zipping all over the globe is not necessarily noble or impressive at all. "Tell us what you have seen," demands the poem's third section, inaugurating a lengthy fourth section full of talk of "the richest towns and finest countrysides," "palaces whose wild luxuriance / would bankrupt all your bankers in their dreams," etc. And then the fifth section is a single line of three questions, two of them the same. I made a copy of it in the library, the better to tape it to the inside of my locker.

And then? And then? What else?

It was a good thing to look at during a crummy school day—a poet skewering a mighty epic with a raised eyebrow and a bit of a yawn, like on the cover my Pet Shop Boys album. This slant was of immense comfort to me. As a teenager I was being told so many things were important—academic achievement, respectful behavior, the mandatory admiration of so much idiocy and all sorts of fools. I tried my best to comply. But still, even when I appeared impeccable, I had the dire, certain feeling that I was dumb and doing it wrong. Baudelaire—and Pet Shop Boys, too—raised the possibility that the grand strictures the world announced were what was dumb, that we were all just casting about blindly.

I was dumb in museums, for instance. I didn't get it. I liked art—some of it—but I didn't like what you had to do when you went to look at it. You had to go wall by wall, gallery by gallery, staring at each artwork for a period of time lengthy enough to indicate, to yourself and others, that you'd absorbed something or other. I didn't like this. I wasn't good at it. It took too long. The only way I could do it was by cheating—by pretending that something in a faraway gallery had suddenly captured my attention with such ferocity that I would stride quickly toward it, thus disrupting the thing I was supposed to be doing, by skipping whole walls full of paintings and such. In that faraway gallery, after a few steady viewings, I would spy something in another faraway gallery and in this way could stepping-stone my way toward things I liked to look at, but even then it was tough, because I would have liked to look at those things for longer. But I had to keep moving. *And then? And then? What else?*

It was my wife, my darling, who taught me that it was OK just to walk into a museum and look at whatever you wanted. On an early date she took me to a place she loved as a child, the Wadsworth Atheneum in Hartford, Connecticut. Like all museums, it's a building full of things, the majority of which do not interest you. She took me only to the things she liked best, a straight unblinking path right to them, something I did not really know was allowed. "These are the facts," goes a Neneh Cherry lyric that's been lurking in my head for years, "and here is the news: I just want you to want it too." In showing me what she liked, my darling was showing me the part of her mind oblivious to the pressures of the world, the little peculiar bits, in order to see if I liked them, too. I did—enough of them, anyway. "No one ever knows what she's laughing about," her best friend told me, after a few such dates, "and we still don't, but now at least there's two of you."

Hardly a week goes by, for instance, without my wife and me singing to each other a song we heard just once, more than twenty years ago, on the day she received her master's from art school. There was an unremarkable outdoor ceremony, and afterward we were milling out of the campus along with other graduates and their families. This being an art school, the campus was littered with sculpture, and my wife and I passed a short metal figure—square head, blocky body with buttons and gears—which was being appreciated by a young boy, perhaps the son of another graduate. He was banging on it and singing along with the resonant clanks, a song he had surely composed himself:

> I am a robot, I am a robot
> I am a robot, I am a robot
> I am a robot, I am a robot
> I am a robot, I am a robot
> I am a robot, I am a robot

As songs go, it's not much. The one-note melody and ultra-repetitive structure would make Philip Glass beg for variety, and the lyrics, after the first couplet, are pretty predictable. I can't imagine the composer remembers it himself. Yet we sing it all the time, and of course I have it written down—it's been written down in notebook after notebook as it reoccurs to me. Many of its neighbors in the notebooks have found their place in my writings, but not

> I am a robot, I am a robot
> I am a robot, I am a robot
> I am a robot, I am a robot
> I am a robot, I am a robot

It has bided its time, like a murderous beadseller, until finally, here, I have use for it. Maybe it is of interest to you. I hope it is; *I just want you to want it too.* But in any case it was freeing to learn that all of the tiny, scrappy things I like were not symptoms of being dumb, or, if they were, at least I could find other dumb people who loved them as much as I did.

I write things down now in the cheapest notebooks I can find, slapdash pocket-sized things so anonymous and flimsy that there's nothing too dumb for their pages. I've kept at it this way, a flood of little things I've noticed, in the world and/or in my own head, snatches of overheard conversations and odd spied sights, language from poetry and placards, isolated bits of memory and imagination and both and neither. I can trace back each of my novels, each *paragraph*, almost, to some stray remark, some small phrase that went the distance and turned into a story. But most of the scraps just sit there dumbly, waiting for their day.

That day may never come—so often these scraps are acts of solitude. I feel certain that nobody from *Murder on the Nile* ever thinks of the Beadsellers murdering the Steward, and it's a little melancholy to be the only one left in the theater, some forty years after the performance. But you never know. When my sister and I were young, we were taken to the Rose Parade, though exactly when and why and who took us is lost. What stays is one of the floats, a whale, exactly one hundred feet long, that both my sister and I saw, and kept in our heads as a handy measure of one hundred feet. For years, she and I conjured up the whale silently in our heads, when something was one hundred feet long, or tall, or away, and then, when we were adults, in one of the great connective moments in my life, joyous and astonishing, when we learned that we were both holding the same scrap in our mind. All of us have something like this in our lives, the parallel coincidence that is astonishing because it puts into precise relief how few of the scraps in our minds are ever shared by someone else.

For a few years, I wrote a column for a magazine about the Nobel Prize in Literature, reading one book by each of the laureates. In preparation, armed with a long list, I wandered all over town to bookshops full of dusty obscurities and startling treats, shops which have educated and delighted me my whole life. But most of the books on my list—books by authors awarded the highest literary prize in the world—were too obscure even for stores selling books nobody reads. This was familiar. I'm usually not reading what other people are reading. I get accused of playing cooler-than-thou—*Me? Oh, I'm reading that Henry Parland book Eliot Weinberger likes*—but the truth of the matter is that I just like this stuff. I like the Scandinavian modernism. I like the self-published queer rants. I like the secondary experimental novelists in translation and the autobiographical verse novels of decades gone by. The only thing I don't like about it is that nobody else is reading it. I don't like that nobody else is reading it because it seems bad for the world, which would be much improved if everyone knew who Eka Kurniawan is. I don't like that nobody else is reading it because then it's hard to find. And I don't like that nobody else is reading it because I don't have anyone to talk to when I've read it myself. It's tough, at a party, to say, "I'm reading this great novel, *Four Frightened People*, by E. Ernot Robertson" with the utter certainty that the other person will just say, after a lengthy sip, "Huh."

A great example of this is François Mauriac, a Nobel laureate who enjoyed a career as a high-profile intellectual in France, particularly after the Second World War, when he would tussle in the pages of various newspapers with Albert Camus, and whose novel *Viper's Tangle* I found for free in a giveaway bin.

It reads, well, like a novel by a public intellectual, in that it's an unbridled, uninterrupted monologue in the service of an idea. The idea is that Monsieur Louis, an aging lawyer, is not pleased with his wife.

> If I have not given you anything on your birthday for years, it is not because I have forgotten; it is by way of revenge. It suffices . . . The last bunch of flowers I received on my birthday, my poor mother plucked it with her deformed hands. She had dragged herself for the last time, despite her weak heart, as far as the rose-walk.

The voice is like this for the duration—cold and woolgathery, with the sort of psychological signposts that probably seemed more subtle at the time. Its unfashionableness is what I like most about it, the opportunity *Viper's Tangle* provides to think about a time in which such unbridled thinking out loud was considered compelling. It was compelling for me, though of course it's not surprising that not a lot of people are reading it. At least one person had read my copy, though. It was an old hardcover, with that used-book smell and a few sticky pages at the back. I unstuck them and a piece of paper fell into my hands. I unfolded it, and in tiny, bygone handwriting covering both sides of the yellowing sheet, I read notes from another reader.

One side of the pages has direct comments on the text, with page notations—the exact kind of notes I was taking for my column. The reader finds a flourish on page 81 a "poor excuse for intro or diversion—perhaps smoother in the French" and finds a description on page 206 a "summation of what he sees in the world." But on the other side of the sheet, the notetaker lists some broader ideas, with the quaint tone of an old-fashioned English teacher:

2 sides as novelist:

Urbane Frenchman who analyzes love with detachment of a metaphysician

devout Roman Catholic who wrestles with sin

Themes

human flesh as ineradicable temptation

romantic love as path to mutual hatred

bourgeois life as a variety of spiritual sloth

free will as man's great burden

Simple plot

Evil a reality with him

"The people I set out to paint are fallen creatures."

I was most intrigued by that quote there at the end. I didn't remember it from the novel, so I thought it might be something Mauriac had said. I lay this old, lost sheet of paper next to my laptop and typed the quote into Google.

I got just two hits—which looks strange in this time when there's chatter about *everything*—and the top one was from the archives of *Time* magazine—a review of a Mauriac's novel *The Loved and the Unloved*, from the October 6, 1952, issue. The "fallen creatures" quote is indeed credited to Mauriac, from an essay appended to the novel. But what struck me was how the review begins:

> As a novelist, François Mauriac has two sides: 1) the urbane Frenchman who analyzes love with the detachment of a metaphysician, and 2) the devout Roman Catholic who wrestles with sin.

Mauriac's latest novel, *The Loved And The Unloved*, rehearses his usual themes: human flesh as ineradicable temptation, romantic love as path to mutual hatred, bourgeois life as a variety of spiritual sloth, and free will as man's great burden.

I looked from the screen to the piece of paper and back again, the identical and unlikely wording a bridge between us, some fifty years apart—the readers of this copy of *Viper's Tangle*. The review is uncredited, and of course it's possible that I read those notes the wrong way round, and that some other lonely reader of *Viper's Tangle* sought out, before the days of web archives, someone else who was thinking about Mauriac, and jotted down *Time* magazine's phrases for their own bookish traipse. But in that moment the whole enterprise of literature shone clear.

Every book begins as someone's private obsession—some dumb little scrap, observed or historical or invented—about which hardly anyone cares a whit but the author. The rest of the world goes about its business and the author sits mulling this tiny thing over, this dumb little irritant pecking at a place unreachable in the skull except by writing things down. *And then*, the book is brought out to an almost invisible conversation. You hope someone is listening, and sometimes—through some reaction bubbling through the overgrown shrubbery of platforms and bullhorns—you might learn that someone is, in fact, looking at the thing you're pointing at. But reading is mostly private. Readers' reactions to words on the page are hardly known to anyone, even sometimes to the reader, let alone to the author, and even a visible reaction—what some reader has *noticed*—is so very unlikely to be sharing the same slant, the same shape, the same fervor of whatever it is the author is interested in saying. Reactions to my own work are on a bafflingly enormous spectrum, across every vector I can imagine and quite a few I can't, and these are just the reactions I know about, which means that my own reactions as a reader are likewise almost always missing some mark the author cannot stop thinking about. *And then*, this is, of course, not limited to literature, not at all. Everyone is milling and mulling around the museum, setting off on a seaward voyage, noting and remembering only some tiny fraction of the adventure in a way that says more about our own peculiarities than those of the world. *What else?*

> Dismay is what one learns from voyaging.
> Today, tomorrow, yesterday, the bland
> world gives us back our own reflection: a spring
> of horror rising out of boring sand!

These dark moments of Baudelaire's, of any author's anxiety that the journey is all for naught, are refuted by anyone reading Baudelaire to begin with—me, for instance. I am not some dumb robot, or a character so minor I couldn't possibly be the murderer. I am connected to something. The more little scraps that resonate with me, the more I know that my own scrappy efforts are, somewhere likely invisible, being chewed over, until the scraps do not seem so little after all, but something quite large and peculiar I can imagine and remember and describe here on paper, even if it's appreciated only by one or two people who for whatever reason are primed to notice it. It's like—and my sister knows what this is like—something enormous, unforgettable, made of flowers, that parades by one blurry day but lingers forever someplace in someone's mind.

13

What is it trying
to tell me?

When my son was small, he woke me up in the middle of
the night with a deafening whisper:

"*Dad. Dad. Dad. Dad. Dad. Dad. Dad. Dad. Dad. Dad. Dad.
Dad. Dad. Dad.*"

I opened my eyes and he led me out of bed to an empty room.
We were renting a house by the beach, and from the window of
this guestless guest bedroom the two of us could see the clear,
circulating beam of a lighthouse across the dark sea and sky.
It was admittedly beautiful, but it was three in the goddamn
morning. My son was a lighthouse fiend. The lighthouse had
been admired many times, from different angles at all kinds
of times of day. But my son wasn't done with it. It kept calling
to him, way past his bedtime, like—well, like a lighthouse. He
jumped up and down beside me, his face flickering as the beam
went by, and asked me a question I've asked myself continually
since, when I am thinking about something that won't let me go.

"*What is it trying to tell me?*"

I told my son that the lighthouse was telling him to go back to bed, which of course was the wrong answer. But there's no explanation I could give him for why that lighthouse held his attention. We see or hear things, we read things and think about them, and they live in our minds, sometimes fiendishly forever and sometimes for hardly any duration at all, prioritized in some way, by some shifting metric unknown to everybody, even—*most of all*—ourselves. Why these things? What are they trying to tell us?

I have the last of my index cards here at the café table, along with two books hardly anyone reads. One is a novel with an awkward title; the other is indescribable, indecipherable even, titled, appropriately, *Hieroglyphics*. Every café has a tragic flaw, and the tragic flaw of this one is that the food is delicious, so I am tempted to order some of it, and spend the next few hours feeling full and content paging through these books. This is no way to write. But my morning took me far from the café whose tragic flaw is a horrendous bathroom, and the one whose tragic flaw is Christmas music all year round, and it's too late in the day for the café whose tragic flaw is closing at 2:30 p.m., or the library branch whose tragic flaw is loud loud loud children after school. So I am here. This café has good tables for working, even though they look small and rickety. You can't tell until you sit down. Once I worked in a café in Vancouver—I was finishing the second draft of *Poison for Breakfast*—which had a beautiful table, grand and spacious, right by a window with lots of light. Only when I sat down did I learn it was stifling hot and buzzing with flies. I moved tables and spent the afternoon watching customer after customer wonder why the best table was vacant, sit down, flinch and shoo, and finally get up and move. Everyone has to learn for themselves. I am still trying to learn how and why I do whatever it is I am doing. I am hoping I can do it. But a sentence like "I am still trying to learn how and why I do whatever it is I am doing" gives me doubt.

Years ago I turned in a draft of a script to a film director for his suggestions and got it back scrawled with the initials *DB* all over the place. "DB?" I said, when I managed to get him on the phone.

"Yes, Danny," he said. Besides one old lady, he is the only one ever to call me this.

"What does 'DB' mean?"

"Do Better."

"Do Better? That's your note?"

"Yes, Danny. The script is pretty bad now. Those parts I marked DB, make them better."

I sputtered something he couldn't have heard, because he hung up. He is an infuriating person, often cruel, frequently dumb, completely untrustworthy, reliably hilarious, lots of fun, a lunatic very good at his job. I'd never encountered more irritating criticism—"criticism" didn't seem the word for it; it felt more like "bullying"—than DB, and now I write it in my own margins all the time, shorthand for *I don't know what's wrong here but it needs to improve*. I want to write better, but I usually don't know how. Nobody does, really. "I write down an absurd sentence," says Paul Valéry, one of my favorite writers, "instead of illuminating insight which shouldn't be grasped or which—wasn't one." This is comforting, but only to an extent. Valery still writes an elegant sentence when he's unable to write an elegant sentence, dammit. He's the sort of fool who is really wise; I'm more the regular kind.

For instance, I'm a fool for a novel by William Maxwell, *Time Will Darken It*, and yes, the title needs work. Among the scenes which stay with me is one in which a man, after a bitter conflict with his wife, takes a fuming walk late at night while she similarly rages around. They return to each other, side by side in bed, and each time I reread the novel and the scene approaches, I can never remember how the couple feels as they return to bed—I remember it, or misremember it, as a scene of quiet reconciliation, or numbing resignation, or the fierce sulk of protracted, possibly doomed distance between them. The answer is yes:

Austin stirred, and put his arm across her, and she took hold of it, by the wrist, and removed it, but when she moved away from him, towards the outer edge of the bed, he followed again in his sleep, and curled around her in a way that made her want to shout at him, and beat his face with her fists. She pushed the arm away, roughly this time, but he still did not waken. The arm had a life of its own. All the rest of him, his body and his soul, were asleep. But the arm was awake, and came across her, and the hand settled on her heart, and she let it stay there for a moment, thinking how hard and heavy it was compared to the child she had been holding, how importunate, how demanding; how it was no part of her and never would be, insisting on a satisfaction, even in sleep, that she could not give. She started to push it away once more but her own arms were bound to the bed. Only her mind was

awake, able to act, to hate. And then suddenly the delicate gold chain of awareness, no stronger than its weakest
link, gave way. Circled by the body next to her, enclosed in
warmth, held by the arm that knew (even though the man
it belonged to did not), Martha King was asleep.

It's a nuanced, contradictory paragraph, a clear-eyed portrait of
people who have been together through a lot for a long time, but
it is never quite how I remember it, despite my profound admiration for this brilliant book. What is it trying to tell me? Even
looking at it again for this chapter, I was surprised, almost as if
the scene had changed once more, since maybe my tenth reading of it. Is this successful literature—a passage so elusive that
even if you're a fiend for it, which I clearly am, you can't quite
nail it down? Is there something wrong with it, that it captivates
without sticking? Or am I really just writing something about
my own mind, which could have picked up any paragraph, like
a favorite pebble?

This brings me to the other book here on the café table nobody
reads: *Hieroglyphics* by Arthur Machen, and no you haven't:

What is it that differentiates fine literature from a number
of grammatical, or partly grammatical sentences arranged
in more or less logical order? Why is the Odyssey to come
in, why is the "literature" or our evening paper to be kept
out? . . . What is the line, then; the mark of division which
is to separate spoken, or written, or printed thought into
two great genera? Well, as you may have guessed, I have
my solution, and I like it none the less because the word

of the enigma seems to me actually but a single word. Yes, for me the answer comes with the one word, *Ecstasy*. If ecstasy be present, then I say there is fine literature; if it be absent, then, in spite of all the cleverness, all the talents, all the workmanship and observation and dexterity you may show me, then, I think, we have a product (possibly a very interesting one) which is not fine literature.

I love how simple, how personal, the definition is—so personal it may not be a definition at all.

It describes the tiny bits which stick with us, which move us; not the whole of some mighty book but some tiny cog that won't leave you alone. I began this book with my finding Baudelaire when I was twelve:

Stupidity, delusion, selfishness and lust
torment our bodies and possess our minds,
and we sustain our affable remorse
the way a beggar nourishes his lice.

but those lines weren't the first things from a book I noticed, of course. As far as I can remember, before I can remember, I loved being read to, and I loved reading, but I also loved just staring at books, thinking about them, trying to figure out—I don't know what—where they were from, the way they worked, how they did it. My first favorite book that I stared at like this, I think, was called *The Bears' Famous Invasion of Sicily*, a forgotten copy of a book out of print and out of mind, old and odd, likely once owned by my great-aunt, who was the same way. The author,

Dino Buzzati, is an Italian writer better known for his eerie, politically pointed work for adults; his only children's book, *The Bears' Famous Invasion of Sicily* is an adventure story about, guess what, some bears invading Sicily, and I spent just as much time rereading the book as I did staring deeply at the illustrations. The full-page color spreads and smaller black-and-white incidentals, rich in details—details the author insists were drawn incorrectly. "Why does the artist play this joke on us?" he interrupts the story to complain, but I still stared at them. The best part was the illustrated list of characters, from King Leander ("a bear of most ancient lineage") to a Screech-Owl ("We will hear his voice for a moment in Chapter Two."), and the best part of the best part was the Werewolf:

> It is possible that he may not appear in our story. In fact, as far as we know he has never appeared anywhere, but one never knows. He might suddenly appear from one moment to the next, and then how foolish we should look for not having mentioned him.

—and a werewolf in fact does not appear in the book. What was this trying to tell me? I could not take my eyes off these three sentences, in a book I knew hardly anyone else was reading. This little thing rattled in my mind like a joke I couldn't wait to tell people, even if nobody got it. (Not until I was an adult would I realize the bigger joke—the illustrator Buzzati complains about is, guess what, himself.)

It is this feeling, this jumpy enthusiasm, this ecstasy, that is at the heart of all literary exercise, so often overlooked in favor of other traits, nobler or easier to articulate. We don't read to become better people, to DB, even if that happens along the way. The reason we read—the reason you're reading this book—is because some other book enchanted you, earlier on, and before that another, and before that another. This is the real literary canon, not some hegemonic pantheon, adapted and debated over time. We each have one, a literary canon, and we make it ourselves, not out of what is respectable or prestigious or prominent or lasting or moral or even well-made. We make it out of enthusiasm, out of what we love. A sustained thread of enthusiasm, to which I try to connect myself, conjuring it up when I'm writing, from the books I have with me, on the table or just in my mind. And not just books. Perhaps my biggest inspiration, my true artistic hero, isn't much of a writer, though he is an endless fountain of such ecstasy.

I was at a noisy party in college, and thought I was hearing two records playing at once. I was standing in a doorway and I moved toward the one I liked better, which had an organ, or maybe a woman singing, while someone played a boozy piano, and away from a violin which was, coincidentally, playing a melody along very similar chords. By the time I was standing near the stereo speaker, all this had merged into something else, something which sounded like an elementary school music class, plunking on gongs, xylophones, while the pianist tried his best to corral it into scraggly order. I hadn't heard any music like that in my entire life, not on a record, anyway. It was noisy, but not in the usual way music got noisy, in order to tick people off, to confront or unnerve them. This was noisy in a more playful way, a happy way, like pitching rocks into the water, or singing in the shower. The pianist was on the cover of the album, wearing a headdress festooned with glitter and antennae and a ring or two, just like Saturn. His name was Sun Ra.

I went out and bought a record, and I keep buying them. The albums are called things like *Art Forms of Dimensions Tomorrow* and *Cosmic Tones for Mental Therapy*, full of songs with titles like "Infinity of the Universe" and "Voice of Space." There is an almost endless supply of them, made with a revolving cast of cohorts called "arkestras," horn players and percussionists, sometimes a singer or an entire orchestra, Sun Ra shepherding them with keyboards of every stripe—pianos and organs, harpsichords and an array of synthesizers buzzing and burping and boinging along.

The premise of his music, if music can be said to have a premise, is that Sun Ra has arrived from outer space to usher in changes to the state we're in—not only easily identifiable problems (bigotry, destruction of the environment) but various unhealthy states of consciousness, which are maybe the same thing. This mission places his music as part of Afrofuturism, a movement loosely grouping various artforms that postulate an imaginary space, far from Earth as we know it, in which Black culture is utterly liberated and liberational—not just a political movement or an aesthetic one but a philosophy in which those are the same. Sun Ra's jazz moves past the standard cool of jazz into—well, into outer space. His music is like his headgear, handmade, spacey, fashioned out of all kinds of things he liked: doowop, funk, disco, experimental noise, chanting from disparate cultures, and old cartoons. He liked Batman a lot, and Duke Ellington. A household favorite is his song "Enlightenment," which begins with a solemn, stagey gong, and then a low, wandering melody, which then, both unexpectedly and inevitably, lopes its way into a dance tune. My wife has told me that I cannot describe, here in these pages, the special dance she does during this part of the song, but surely the important thing here is that she has a special dance for it in the first place.

Listening to this song brings happiness to my household—it changes our consciousness. This—not my description of it, but *this*—is what I want to do in literature. Hearing his music, simultaneously old-timey and space-age, reminds me of all the clutter I've had in my head forever, which, following Sun Ra's example, traipses through various philosophical landscapes in my mind to land on the page, I hope, accessibly and harmoniously.

Almost forty years ago, in high school, for instance, we were all required to take a three-pronged career test: first we chose, from an excruciatingly long list of choices, professions that interested us; then they told us, from some dubious metric, what we might be good at; then, faced with the same list again, we had to indicate if we'd changed our minds. My friend and I convinced our homeroom, during this last step, to leave unchecked each career on the list, and then to check "other," and in the blank provided write "pirate." This got me in trouble, of course—I was told, implausibly, that this had thrown off the entire statistical analysis for the state of California—but I kept the idea in my head: fed-up teenagers who want to be pirates. It waited in a corner of my mind, like a lurking werewolf, or a sticky tune. I wanted two girls, furious and fun like my sister, as the heroes, rather than the usual strapping young men. An old man would lead them, I thought, years later, although I couldn't figure out why this old man would do such a thing, until, years later again, my father's dementia began to manifest itself in rash, sometimes fierce acts, but always smilingly, joyfully and often, to those who did not know him well, convincingly sane. The freakish idea, *pirates*, became sadder, more desperate, more violent. I reread favorite novels that seemed relevant—Richard Hughes's always astonishing *A High Wind In Jamaica*, Marianne Wiggins's *John Dollar*, and watched pirate movies with index cards piled up nearby. My father faltered and faded, and I lay that part of him to rest, some years after he died, in my novel *We Are Pirates*, along with the high school prank and countless other tiny ecstatic items. All my books are like this, corralled together from things I've been mulling over for years. It is a quiet feeling, when I find a place for them. I think of Odysseus, sort of a pirate, getting home at last toward the end of the *Odyssey*:

> They rowed inside the bay; they knew the place
> of old. Their arms were pulling at top speed;
> the ship was traveling so fast that when
> she reached dry land, she beached for half her length.
> They disembarked, and lifted from the ship
> Odysseus, wrapped up in sheets and blankets.
> They set him on the sand, still fast asleep.
> They unpacked all the presents he was given
> by the Phaeacian lords to take back home,
> thanks to Athena's care. They heaped the things
> beside the olive tree, so no one passing

would do them any damage while their owner
was sleeping. Then they rowed away, back home.

—or perhaps that's just because I have an index card reading
"Odysseus coming home Emily Wilson translation" stacked
with the *Hieroglyphics* card because Machen mentions the *Odyssey*, too. It feels like the right description of what I'm getting
at, the arrival of literature from the mind of the writer. In this
whole book I've tried to lay out my canon for anyone who might
be interested, little pieces entangled necessarily with little pieces
of my life, because of this ecstasy.

The luckiest part of my literary life is sometimes getting to
see my own work arrive and settle into readers' minds. This usually happens in private, of course, but not when you're young,
not always. For a book of mine called *Goldfish Ghost*, about a
lonely dead goldish floating around upside down, I went on book
tour with the illustrator, who happens to be my wife—although
it felt illicit to keep checking into hotels together. When we
presented the book in various elementary school auditoriums,
I would again serve as Lemony Snicket's representative, and
explain that Mr. Snicket had failed to show up because he was
lonely. "If he's lonely," Lisa Brown would ask me, "why doesn't he
come here, where there are a lot of charming people?"

"He likes being lonely," I'd say, "he's a loneliness savant,"
and would explain that *savant* was a word which here means
somebody really good at something. The rest of us, I said,
needed more practice. We all sat together doing it, the people
who had made the book and the people having it read to them,

in the same quiet space. It is so easy to forget to be lonely, the way it is so easy to forget to read. It is the whole point of the enterprise, to make something from which someone else might take something else.

When I started writing this book, I'd just seen something I couldn't stop thinking about. It was a time of unrest in my country. Vicious and senseless violence, ongoing and impossible to swallow, had prompted fervent, furious protests, which in turn brought more destruction and more heartbreak. A young woman stood in front of a wrecked storefront, and her boyfriend took a photograph of her, posed provocatively, to be posted online. Someone else had filmed the boyfriend photographing her, and posted that, and now everyone in this little piece of screen was furious. I sat staring and felt something falling away from me, nicked off in little layers. The protests and what prompted them, the destruction, the woman posing, her boyfriend taking the picture, whoever it was who put all this up, whoever I was looking at it. It was a familiar, wrecking loss. The mess, the horrendous mess, such ghastly images, such shattered stories, the opposite of the comfort of literature I've had the privilege of enjoying since childhood. Stupidity, delusion and selfishness tormented my body and possessed my mind. I did not know how to fix anything, but I wanted to write DB in the margin of the world.

You know what this is; I know you do. It almost doesn't matter exactly what it was I was staring at; you can substitute whatever it is you saw that horrified you. How can such a loss be comforted, how can it be repaired? You must—*we* must—build it back the same way, layer by layer, out of tiny things we find and love. I've used up all my index cards on this last chapter, stuffed it with all these little things while making this thing for you, because I know, through literature and through life, I can always find more to love. So, so much has been written down, and I write this down for the same reason: in the hopes of bringing ecstasy, to the next reader, as so many writers have done for me.

ACKNOWLEDGMENTS

T^K TK

APPENDIX

I mention many books in this book, along with quite a few movies and pieces of music. Obviously I recommend them all, but it is possible you have a life of your own, so here is a reduced list of thirteen things I mentioned only briefly, which I particularly enjoy recommending.

Busby Berkeley, *The Gang's All Here*.

Simultaneously one of the most bonkers and most conventional films you can see, and thus a reminder that the normal and the peculiar are eternally intertwined.

Heather Christle, *The Trees The Trees*.

A wonderful poetry collection with terrific titles. When I want to think about titles I turn to Heather Christle, who has also written an excellent book about crying.

Duke Ellington, soundtrack to *Anatomy of a Murder*.

The film's terrific but the music is a sublime and sneaky parade of a variety of emotional tones. I dislike thinking of music as narrative—I think music's lack of narrative qualities is often its most charming attribute—but I do like how Ellington leads me around.

Ralph Ellison, *Invisible Man*.

It is interesting to me how canonization often makes people forget how individual and peculiar so many classics are. This book is more strange and more wondrous than you might remember, and if you have been put off reading it because of its iconic status—well, don't be.

Rachel Ingalls, *Mrs. Caliban*.

A quiet love story involving a monster, a small marvel of a book from perhaps my favorite author.

Guy Maddin, *Careful*.

A melodrama taking place in an entirely new world, yet one that feels like something you saw, perhaps when you were very young, on a screen someplace.

Haruki Murakami, *A Wild Sheep Chase*, in Alfred Birnbaum's translation.

In some ways, Murakami is a mirror-image of Ellison—a highly visible author whose strangeness is exaggerated. Curious things happen in his novels, but they are so plainly described and so easily digested that we're reminded curiosity is omnipresent.

Henry Parland, *Ideals Clearance*, in Johannes Göransson's translation.

Tiny and tidy poems from a Finn who wrote in Swedish. I turn to this book when I want to think about little words.

Prince, *The Black Album*.

Explicit filth, utterly convincing.

Muriel Spark, *Not to Disturb*.

Another small marvel of a book, which starts as a familiar mystery and moves into hilarious and devilish territory. It is a perfect book to buy for someone else because it is so short that you know they will read it.

Lou Sullivan, *We Both Laughed in Pleasure*.

A diary to read and be reminded of how utterly unpredictable, how *unseeable*, one's life is.

Sun Ra, *Sound Sun Pleasure!!*

Utter joy, with some rough edges, the way joy behaves. I try to be open to the limitless variety of people's tastes, but quite honestly if you do not like this record I think something is wrong with you.

Nafkote Tamirat, *The Parking Lot Attendant*.

One of my favorite recent novels, which sits with the inexplicability of the world and thinks about the infinite ways one can be an outsider—and thus an insider, too.

And I cannot resist recommending these other thirteen things which are not otherwise mentioned in this book:

The 6ths, *Hyacinths and Thistles.*

My favorite collection of Stephin Merritt's songs, featuring a lovely array of singers and an accordionist modesty prevents me from mentioning.

Chris Adrian, *The Children's Hospital.*

An oft-overlooked masterpiece and a rip-roaring read, one of the secret greatest novels of the fairly new twenty-first century.

Victoria Chang, *The Boss.*

Poems of fierce argument and a sharp and stumbly diction. I return to this book when I need reminding of how to shuffle words around.

J. P. Donleavy, *The Lady Who Liked Clean Restrooms.*

A slight comedy, a perfect plot.

Tom Drury, *The Black Brook.*

Maybe my favorite book in the world, deadpan and melancholy, incisive and wondering, with new things to notice wherever you go.

Morton Feldman, *Crippled Symmetry.*

A long, quiet piece of music which nonetheless percolates with suspense and curiosity. I listen to this and think about how effective small movements can be.

Barry Gifford, *The Stars Above Veracruz.*

A truly remarkable collection of stories, zippy and thoughtful, varied but hanging out well together, as if in a good bar.

Alberto Gout, *Aventurera*.

A melodramatic film that zigs and zags its way across story, genre and tone, staking a claim that entertainment and sense are perhaps direct opposites. Also, it is a musical.

Lillian Hellman, *Maybe*.

A loopy and completely unreliable memoir of sorts—a rant, a ramble, with all the startle of realizing that none of us really remember anything the way it happened, because there is no such thing.

Cheon Myeong-kwan, *Whale*, in Chi-Young Kim's translation.

A terrific epic, an enormous metaphor for something I can't quite delineate, but I keep feeling its shadow. This book is following me, I think.

Horacio Castellanos Moya, *Dance with Snakes*, in Lee Paula Springer's translation.

It is useful to know where the edges are. This novel is there. It is a phantasmagorical political allegory and a police procedural.

Morgan Parker, *Other People's Comfort Keeps Me Up at Night*.

A collection of poems, both breezy and searing to read, that helps me think about voice—the way unity and difference, even duplicity, will not just emerge from the same source but in fact be its identifying characteristics.

Mark Robson, *The Seventh Victim*.

This film, even alongside others produced by the notorious and mysterious Val Lewton, is so bewildering I do not even know what to say about it. Perhaps someday we will meet to discuss the matter.

and

Charles Baudelaire, *The Flowers of Evil*, in both Aaron Poochigian's and Richard Howard's translations.

Don't get me started.